50 Years of Modern Art

50 Years of Modern Art

Introduction by Emile Langui

32 color plates

305 monochrome illustrations

226 biographical notes

Frederick A. Praeger, Publishers **New York**

BOOKS THAT MATTER

Published in the United States of America in 1959
by Frederick A. Praeger, Inc., Publishers
15 West 47th Street, New York 36, N.Y.
All rights reserved
Library of Congress catalog card number: 59-7300
Printed in Germany
Translated from the French by Geoffrey Sainsbury
and James Oliver
© in Germany 1959 by M. DuMont Schauberg Cologne

Contents

Acknowledgements

This book owes its existence to the world-wide response accorded to the exhibition of "50 Years of Modern Art" which formed a part of the Brussels World Exhibition of 1958. Its contents are here reproduced in permanent form, for the benefit both of those who enjoyed the exhibition and of those who had no opportunity of visiting it. Only a world exhibition of this stature could bring together such a large selection of works of art under one roof and present such a comprehensive picture of the history of art over the last half century.

The selection of exhibits was made by the Belgian Executive Committee in close association with an international committee of experts from the individual countries concerned, whose assistance we gratefully acknowledge:

Belgian Executive Committee

Marquis de la Boëssière-Thiennes, President; †M. Paul Fierens, Chief Curator of the Musées Royaux des Beaux-Arts de Belgique, Vice-President; M. Robert Giron, Director General of the Société Auxiliaire des Expositions du Palais des Beaux-Arts, Vice-President; M. Emile Langui, Director General of Art, Letters and Education, Secretary General; M. Marcel Florkin, Professor of the University of Liège, Belgian delegate to UNESCO; †M. F. M. Olbrechts, Chief Curator of the Musée Royal du Congo Belge, Tervueren; M. Walter Vanbeselaere, Chief Curator of the Musée Royal des Beaux-Arts, Antwerp.

International Committee of Experts

Mr. Mikhaïl Alpatov, Member of the Soviet Academy of Fine Arts
Mr. Cevad Menduh Altar, Director General of Fine Arts, Turkey
Mr. Gino Bacchetti, Head of Department of the Ministry of Antiquities and Fine Arts, Italy
Mr. Oto Bihalji-Merin, Art critic, Belgrade
Mr. Jean Cassou, Chief Curator of the Museum of Modern Art, Paris
Mr. Guglielmo De Angelis d'Ossat, Director General of Antiquities and Fine Arts, Italy
†Mr. Diogo de Macedo, Director of the Museum of Contemporary Art, Lisbon

Mr. Dimitrios Evanguelidis, Professor of the Polytechnic School, Athens

Mr. Fernando Gamboa, Mexico

Sir Philip Hendy, Director of the National Gallery, London

Mr. Atsua Imaizumi, Director of the National Museum of Modern Art, Tokio

Mr. Francisco Iniguez Almech, Director General of the National Art Collections, Spain

Mr. Canon Lanotte, Curator of the Diocesan Museum, Namur

Mr. Kurt Martin, Director General of the Bavarian State Collections of Paintings, Munich

Mr. Vinzenz Oberhammer, Director General of the Museum of Art History, Vienna

Sir Herbert Read, Great Britain

Jonkheer D. C. Roëll, Director General of the Rijksmuseum, Amsterdam

Mrs. Nathalie Sokolova, Corresponding member of the Soviet Academy of Fine Arts

Mr. Georges W. Staempfli, New York

Mr. Michel Stoffel, painter, Luxemburg

Mr. Jan Tomes, Director of the Modern Art Department of the Narodni Gallery, Prague

Mr. John Walker, Director of the National Gallery of Art, Washington

Mr. L.J.K. Wijsenbeek, director of the Fine Arts Department, The Hague

The success of this undertaking is due to these committees and the generosity of those who made the exhibits available – directors of museums, collectors and artists. The significance of the exhibition, hence also of this book, cannot be better expressed than in the final words of the introduction to the exhibition catalogue:
'The highest commendation which our efforts can receive is the approval of the public. Our aim is to reach, not a small number of initiates, as in previous years, but the public at large. For this project, conceived as both an initiation into the art of today and an evaluation of the various aesthetic achievements of our time, is also an overwhelmingly convincing testimony to the essential unity of the human spirit.'

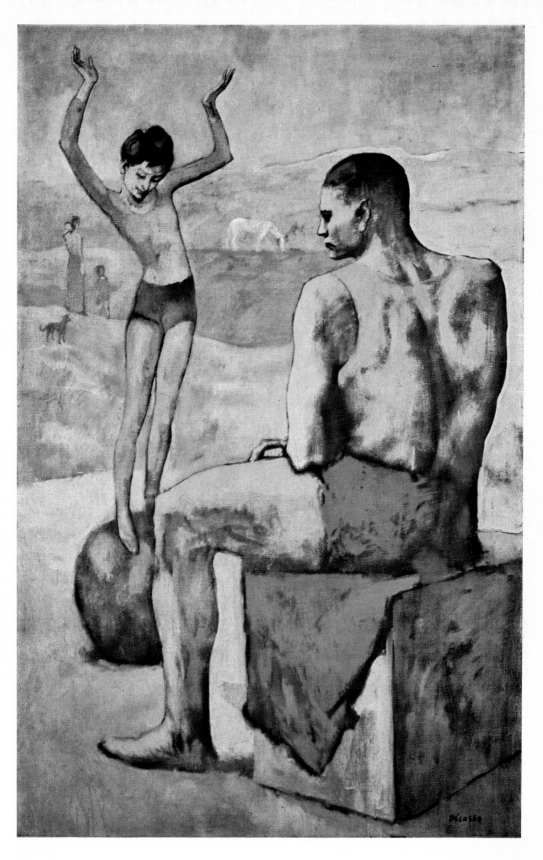

Pablo Picasso, 1939.   255

Introduction

Modern art is as old as man – forty thousand years old, according to Sir Herbert Read, one of the first scholars to have drawn attention to the disturbing resemblance between the majority of contemporary works and those created by mankind at the beginning of time. Nearly all the artistic movements of the past fifty years, however modern, either had their beginning in the distant past or numbered forerunners in remote civilisations. It was the revered traditions of the 19th century and, more broadly, the ancient civilisations of Greece and Rome which made a violent and lamentable break with the past; it is modern art which, beyond all question, has renewed a link with widespread traditions which date back for thousands of years.

Yet there is no need to go back to prehistory, or to seek out primitive peoples in the jungle, in order to find the great pioneers of contemporary art. The 19th century itself brought them into being, though much against its will, though neglecting or exiling them, though condemning them to struggles of intellect and creation outside the limits of conventional society. The so-called failures, the ill-starred, the rebels, madmen and suicides of 'the good old days' fashioned out of their own tragic lives the foundation for what Van Gogh had glimpsed when he said: 'I foresee an art of youth and beauty in the future'.

This is far from claiming that the painting and sculpture of these forerunners were only the first fruits of what was later to surpass them. Their masterpieces have a life of their own, supremely indifferent to any consequences, however illustrious. But the greatness of their influence is all the more striking because the accredited masters of Impressionism seemed to have been cast for this rôle. Yet in reality modern art was born of a revolt against the spiritual inadequacy and the deficiencies of form in the Impressionist style: it was too sensual, too superficial, too inconsistent; and some strong characters, visionaries of forceful temperament, could only find satisfaction by reacting against these tendencies.

There was no organized revolt or deliberate counter-attack among the Impressionists. The independents withdrew of their own accord, in their desire to concentrate the technique and deepen the meaning of Luminism: Cézanne by his sense of composition and construction, Seurat by disciplining his emotion, Van Gogh by his human qualities, Gauguin by synthesis, Munch by his dramatic sense,

Holder by a monumental element in his work, Maillol by recourse to classicism, Bonnard by intimacy, and Ensor by fantasy.

Impressionism itself was far enough away from objective realism – think of Claude Monet's *Water Lilies*! – for a few outstanding men, hardly more than a dozen, to be able to take the final step and enter the great regions of the unreal, the intellectual, the fantastic – even the abstract.

Modern Art did not drop from the skies like some *deus ex machina*, as improbable as it is inevitable. The evolution of the plastic arts from Cézanne up to the present day has been a *logical* sequence of long and laborious conquests, some temporary, some final, some achieved in order, some in anarchy; but all of them, though fiercely individualist, bear the mark of a vital human message, like a sort of contemporary epic sung or shouted in the frightening rhythm of our age.

Yet there is still in existence a kind of intellectual malice which seeks to make trouble between 'those artists' and mankind as a whole by declaring that the absence of the human face necessarily leads to the absence of humanity. If the likeness of man is often absent from modern art, Man himself is present, whole and naked – more so than in any academic nudes.

'Signs have taken the place of objects', said Jean Cassou. That is also true of Man, for soul and intellect have abolished anatomy.

Fauvism

When Matisse put forward his statement that 'in looking at a painting one has to forget what it represents', he laid down a principle which applies to almost the whole of modern art. But he was probably only thinking of his own and his friends' – the Fauves painting. That does not alter the fact that he and they started the first conscious and decisive movement in the arts of the modern period.

It is true that the Fauves owed much to Cézanne, Van Gogh, and Munch, and an immense amount to Gauguin, but it was they and their German comrades of the *Brücke* who, from 1905 onwards, deliberately shifted the centre of Western art by using themes to express their subjective outlook.

Georges Braque, 1913.   38

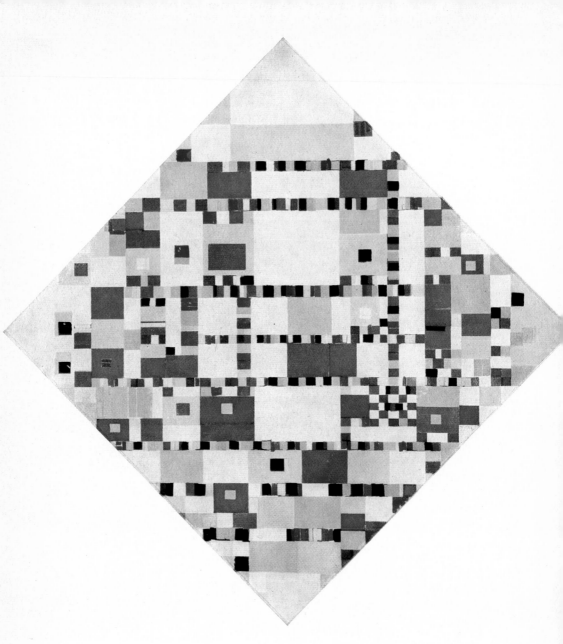

Piet Mondrian, 1943/1944.

Paris and Dresden together rejected Luminism no less than academic art by claiming a complete freedom in plastic creation. From that moment the fact of the painting took the place of the fact in real life. It was far more a psychological than a visual change. While sharing the optimism and exuberance of the Impressionists, the Fauves aimed at making something more solid, less momentary. No longer content simply to make a composition of nature, they built it up as arbitrarily as the Cubists were to construct it two or three years later. Yet the Cubists had the benefit of a severe and systematic body of doctrine, while the Fauves in their sensual lyricism neglected reason.

The Fauves, whether they were Latin, German, Scandinavian, or Slav, painted according to their instinctive feeling for life. They transformed their exuberance into clear and distinct qualities, into strength and greatness. A uniform brilliance replaced the Impressionist play of light and atmosphere. The Fauves brought back rhythm in line, outlines which define objects, a smooth style which can express form and light together. Their palette was limited to a range of definite colours dominated by green, orange, blue, brick-red, and violet. Harmony of contrasts was carried to an extreme, but the effect was both sober and distinguished. Rhythm and colour-combinations took precedence over all matters of perspective and form.

Bound neither by forms nor by colours as they appear in the real world, the Fauve painter drew from the object what his artistic symphony required and did not hesitate to introduce into his composition, for example, a blue or purple horse (Franz Marc) if the laws of counterpoint demanded its presence. Fauve arabesques insinuated themselves into a painting with complete freedom, quite independent of colour. Colour often exceeded the outline, and with Dufy it even came about that the outline was marked a with splash of colour quite distinct from its form.

Fauve painting had elements of charm, decoration, and symbolism and was less concerned with those of the moral, philosophical, or social order – in opposition to some other modern tendencies which have more spiritual depth yet do not attain such wealth of colour.

It is noticeable that Fauvism in France became an end in itself, and the great French masters remained faithful to it up to the end of their careers (Matisse, Dufy, Marquet, Vlaminck, Van Dongen) despite some Expressionist developments (Derain, Vlaminck) which only Rouault carried to a magnificent conclusion. The Germans of the *Brücke* on the other hand (Kirchner, Schmidt-Rottluff, Nolde,

Heckel, Pechstein, and Mueller) soon turned to Expressionism, which had been foreshadowed before 1908 by Paula Modersohn-Becker. In the same way the Fauve period was only a brief prelude to Expressionism for the second German group of the *Blaue Reiter* (Marc, Macke, Klee, Kandinsky, Feininger, and Jawlensky). As for Klee and Kandinsky, and the independent, Rohlfs, by 1912 they had already reached the frontiers of abstract art.

Cubism

Fauvism, as a coherent movement, went on with ups and downs until the outbreak of the first World War. But in reality its positions had already been taken over, in the years 1907–1908, by its own left wing, the Cubists. The same fate, four years later, was to befall the *Brücke*, overwhelmed by the Munich *Blaue Reiter* group.

Yet Cubism represented a swift evolution towards an extremely logical solution of the Fauves' problem. Those who broke away profited from the Fauves' experiments, as the Fauves in turn benefited from the Cubists. It was an intellectual difference, far more than an ordinary aesthetic debate. The Cubists – Braque, Picasso, Gris, Villon, Marcoussis, de La Fresnaye, etc. – entirely rejected lyrical feeling as the first impulse towards the construction of a painting. Their principle was 'the rule of controlled feeling' as against the former doctrine of feelings superior to all rules. The fact that a dose of Cartesian logic was injected into the arts – Cubism could only have come into being in France – was of the greatest consequence for the evolution of 20th century architecture, painting, and sculpture. This fact was decisive for the rise and development of abstract and geometric art.

Closer to Cézanne than to Gauguin, closer to Seurat than to Van Gogh, the Cubists had realised that Fauve painting was still, after all, a somewhat uncertain combination of visual and sensual elements. They themselves meant to put construction first and to keep the emotions well in check. To them reality was primarily a plastic construction of forms, not splashes of colour. Richness of colour

Kasimir Malevitch, 1915.   188

17

Marc Chagall, 1911. 57

Georges Rouault, 1906. 270

Wassily Kandinsky, 1925. 14.

was to them – at least in the beginning – quite a minor consideration. They banished all the chief colours from their palette, keeping only neutral shades, grey, black, coffee, and a blend of green. Their first consideration was the conquest of form, austerely planned according to their own subtle and complicated geometry. Form, once achieved, became increasingly rigid, abstract, and generalised. The third dimension of depth was suggested by an interplay of planes and shadows and by the ingenious use of equilibrium. Protruding angles, sharp edges, everything which drew attention to structure was emphatically accentuated. On the other hand, such things as atmosphere, curved lines, subject, local colour, which serve no purpose in construction, were deliberately rejected. The discovery of African sculpture and negro masks strengthened the Cubists' faith and was used to justify their daring. Indirectly 20th century sensibility was enriched by a taste for the art of so-called primitive peoples.

Such austerity in working out a style soon became hard to sustain, and after its heroic period of analysis Cubism went through many changes and alterations. Its second period brought back the curved line – but it had to be dispassionate! – employed a wider range of colour, granted a larger role to the interplay of light and shade, and renounced geometric extremes. Objects were no longer shown piecemeal, but revealed in several aspects according to different angles of vision.

Later still, to make up for the austerity of their subjects, the Cubists enhanced their work with a mosaic of features and an immense variety of spots of colour. Finally there was the period when Cubism extended freely into space, creating depth by a system of planes in parallel grouping, using strongly opposed colours, subjects, and techniques. But the composition itself always had to retain its balanced charm and its static quality.

It is noticeable that this was the phase – 1914–15 – when the Cubists made use of *collage*, introducing ready-made materials such as coloured or brown paper, wallpaper, corrugated cardboard, string, and bits of stuff into their paintings, gouaches, and drawings. This was less a material protest against theory than an attempt to exalt the commonplace by using the magic of paint to give it a sophisticated appeal. Some years later the Dadaists made great use of this Cubist process, but for the purpose of nihilism.

There is no logical sequence in the evolution of Cubism. Often it has taken up experiments neglected in previous years or made raids into territories outside its own – the rococo, classical, and Ingres periods of Picasso, Braque's caryatids, etc.

Yet this austere art has never lost its contact with reality, which has allowed it to judge all its past experiments and even to reject those conquests which had the greatest appeal. Although it had defined itself as a contemplative form of art, it still had its roots in nature and life. It was by breaking off those roots that it gave birth to abstract art, or at least to one aspect of non-representational art.

The fact that Cubism was able to sum up its aesthetic creed in set terms explains how it has spread all over the world, which in itself brings a risk of swift exhaustion and degeneration into yet another form of academic art. Many talented painters cannot take the place of a few men of genius.

Futurism

Futurism developed in Italy as a parallel movement to Cubism; it had the same impulse to put forward a system, and in some ways tried to imitate it.

Born in Milan and christened in Paris in 1909, it swiftly spread over Italy and a part of Western Europe as a political, social, and artistic rebellion against the past as a whole, against everything that was 'out of date'.

The Futurist Manifesto declared its hatred for the classical conception of beauty, its intention to destroy ancient cities and set fire to museums and libraries. It had no more use for rationalism than for scholasticism. Beauty was only to be achieved by an effort, a struggle. Poetry should be aggressive enough to cause riots, revolutions, even wars. Patriotism and militarism represented man's highest virtues, but the really heroic deed, the proof of merit, was that of the anarchist when he threw a bomb. Killing received the greatest applause.

Futurists thought nothing of women, and nude studies had no place in their aesthetic outlook. Men of their age, which was the age of speed, science, and technics, they flung themselves madly upon life; they had a detestation of thinking, dreaming, or standing still. They tried to live dangerously and were inspired by the beauty of electricity, automobiles, and aircraft.

Apart from its hollow and offensive terminology which confused action with making trouble and life with causing a disturbance, the Futurist Manifesto, coming

Emil Nolde, 1912.   241

as it did at the beginning of the age of technics, seemed like an act of faith asserted by youth in revolt – a perverse pessimism expressing itself in a frenzy of action, movement, and life.

Futurists rejected all earlier styles of art, Cubism among them, because they were essentially static. In opposition to this, their painting and sculpture was based on two dynamic ideas – the motion of bodies in space and the motion of souls in bodies. To achieve this, the artist tried to bring the onlooker into the picture and to give him a physical feeling of dynamic action. With this in view, Futurist painters made use of a system of optical illusions they had invented, based on visual phenomena which had been confirmed by photography and by the cinema. Strong lines and planes gave the cinema's illusion of genuinely moving objects, employing energy and gathering speed in space. The great thing was to suggest, not reality in itself, but reality transformed by motion. This resulted in forms losing all their solidity, as they were dispersed in a kaleidoscope of points, lines and colours. In this way Futurism drew near to Neo-Impressionism, from which it borrowed the stippling process, though using it on a larger scale.

Futurism had very little influence on artists on the other side of the Alps, though it was of great importance to the spread of modern art in Italy. Its theories had hardly any lasting effects on the continent, and what influence it had on Expressionism (Marc, Feininger, Macke, Permeke) came more from its technique than from its inner spirit. It was very soon to lose its greatest artist, Boccioni, who died in 1917, and it was deserted after six or seven years by its best exponents, Carra, Russolo, and Severini, so that Futurist painting did not survive the 1914–18 war. The paradox was that it was the movement's intellectual collapse which brought it to an end, though it had been founded on a cult of life and instinct.

Expressionism

Expressionism ranks among the most important of the modern movements which have overwhelmed the last of Luminism and academic realism, both in the depth and in the extent of its influence. It is much more than a style, for it is a conception of life and a vision of the world seen 'from the inside' – man imposing himself on nature, on events, and on himself.

Cubists and Futurists had already turned aside from objective reality; Expressionists shut their eyes to what they saw and painted intellectually – 'the things one knows more than the things one sees', as Picasso said. The psychological image was what counted, not the visual impression. Thought and creation had to be entirely original, arbitrary, intuitive, without any sort of system, impelled solely by the artist's will and temperament. Whatever the subject – still life, portrait, or landscape – an Expressionist painting in the first place represents the man who painted it, his personal confession.

Consequently there are as many techniques of Expressionism as there are painters in that style. Yet, although they have no one theory in common, they all seem instinctively to accept some law which gives a surprising unity to the movement as a whole.

Expressionists readily yield to the most violent and unconventional promptings of instinct. They are most at home in the deepest and most disturbing mysteries of the soul. In the same way they regard nature and life as being under the sway of a confused tumult of forces which often bring disaster and always bring drama. The artist becomes a sort of hypnotist and his work of art a medium controlled by his own highly charged powers.

Expressionist art is direct, impulsive, rapid, and its passion often attains a kind of ecstasy. Even when he confines himself to an intellectual sketch of his subject, the Expressionist painter usually retains his monumental sense, for any sort of meanness or pettiness is quite alien to his primitive impulse.

Even more than with the Fauves, the line employed by Expressionists is entirely dominated by feeling: it may be strained and rigid, fantastic and uncontrolled, calm and joyful, but it is more often quick, nervous, anguished. As for colour, this is simply a very intense expression of the painter's psychological state with a natural attraction towards the darker shades from deep black to emphatic brown, suddenly broken by flashes of yellow and violet, red and green, blue and orange, applied in daring and frenzied contrasts.

The Expressionists' use of colour found inspiration in the boldness of the Fauves and the *Brücke* artists, but they also drew on such forerunners as Gauguin, Munch, Van Gogh, Redon, Toulouse-Lautrec, Ensor, and Hodler. A swift fusion was brought about by the interaction of painters from Germany, France, Scandinavia,

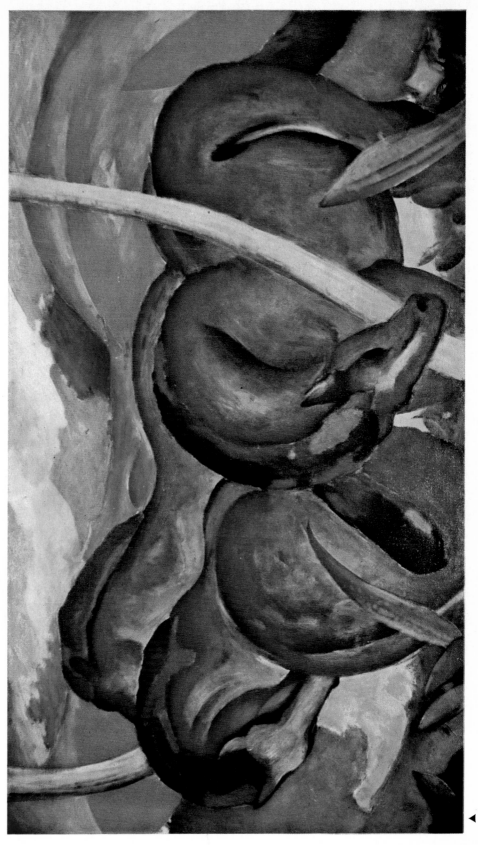

Franz Marc, 1911.   192

Chaïm Soutine, 1928.

Amedeo Modigliani, 1917.   222

Max Beckmann, 1940.

Flanders, Austria, Holland and Russia. In consequence of this, Expressionism spread quickly over all northern and central Europe, then took root in Mexico (Rivera, Orozco, Tamayo, Siqueiros) in the United States (Ben Shahn, De Kooning) and in Brazil (Portinari, Segall).

This fusion remained a constant process, for Expressionism is in essence a mixture of Nordic melancholy, Slav mysticism, Flemish robustness, Jewish anguish, and every sort of Germanic obsession. The German contribution had a decisive effect on its evolution. On the other hand, artists of Latin origin, with a few distinguished exceptions – Rouault, Grommaire, and Picasso in certain aspects – have remained hostile to its romantic or baroque exuberances, its barbaric rejection of all culture, its lack of distinction, and its unpleasant mania for everywhere destroying recognised standards of beauty.

Although Expressionism includes some brilliant minds, to whom we are indebted for many clear treatises on art, the movement in essence remains an explosive display of energy which is necessarily self-destructive. Yet despite its anti-spiritual side and its rejection of any ethical system, it is the strongest effort yet made by the human soul in its domination of the created world. Obsessed by their longing for a nature and a society still in a state of innocence, the Expressionists have discovered and explored the lost paradise of prehistoric and primitive art.

Apart from the forerunners already mentioned, of whom Gauguin, Van Gogh, and Munch are undoubtedly the most important, the Expressionist movement includes a few great independent artists – Rohlfs, Modersohn-Becker, Barlach, Hofer, and Kokoschka – who left their mark on its earliest style and imparted to it some of their mysticism. Oskar Kokoschka and Barlach, no less than Nolde, represent the most striking examples of this trend.

Expressionism came into being at Munich and Berlin at the same moment, about 1910, when the *Blaue Reiter* group took the lead from the *Brücke*, whose best exponents went over to it, while keeping their own apocalyptic outlook. Curiously enough the young *Blaue Reiter* rebels seem today considerably more conventional than their elders. Apart from Beckmann, Expressionism shows its real power in Nolde, Kirchner, Heckel, Schmidt-Rottluff and others of the older generation. The *Blaue Reiter* artists interpreted it much more subjectively. Their concern with 'pure form' and the influence of the Dessau *Bauhaus* split the movement into a number of individualist branches. After that there was no longer a school, only outstanding painters. Soon there was no formal link between the styles of Kandinsky, Feininger, Klee, and Jawlensky, so little connection that several of them brought into being other trends which could no longer be described as Expressionist. All the *Blaue Reiter* group had a tendency towards abstract art which by 1913 had already given birth to a non-representational Expressionism. Klee's genius inspired this movement with such a plastic and poetic breadth that its effects are still being felt today.

Apart from this, the disasters of 1918, the Bolshevist revolution, and the Spartacist rising had affected a number of young Expressionists who had left the trenches with a reawakened social conscience, which clearly marked them off from their comrades who had no political interests.

This was the time when Barlach and Käthe Kollwitz produced their most moving sculptures and engravings, while Grosz and Dix, of the younger generation, started Verism which simply showed the intensity of a brutal realism bent on vengeance. Robbed of all his illusions, the artist in cold anger attacked and unmasked those who were held responsible for the war and social injustice. The Verists, though they made use of Expressionist draughtsmanship and colour, differed in their opinions on the ends served by art. For Grosz and his friends, art had to obey a practical theory, not an artistic ideal. So they were the first to raise the decisive question of 'committed art'.

A few years after it had got rid of its destructive anger, which bore traces of the pre-war Futurist outlook, Verism turned to a hard objective realism, on the model of 16th century German masters. This is the form in which it has survived among many artists of our own day. Another development away from Expressionism, at the same time as Verism, was *Die Neue Sachlichkeit*, or Magic realism. The two branches are often confused. Yet *Neue Sachlichkeit* was a purely objective, even reflective, art which obeyed nature without inflicting on it any disturbing passion or emotional violence. Magic realism controlled any subjective impulse by choosing its themes among the acts and objects of daily life, which were represented with direct and meticulous care, although not without tenderness. Its artists employed a sophisticated and controlled line, bright and positive colours, balanced rhythm. This devotion to truth and respect for life had nothing in common with naturalism. Painting achieved a mysterious and magic poetry, by means of the intellect, light, and especially by the unexpected grouping of miscellaneous objects – recalling the mysterious atmosphere of Chirico's Surrealism. Magic realism was related to Neo-Classicism, but without its reactionary character.

Pablo Picasso, 1905. 250

Constant Permeke, 1928.

Alongside *Neue Sachlichkeit* a monumental and decorative style arose out of Expressionism, best represented by the work of Schlemmer and the earlier Baumeister.

Constructivism and Suprematism

Constructivism was a reaction against the excesses of both Expressionism and Cubism. It demanded a greater objectivity from the artist, to be achieved not by a simple acceptance of reality but by interpreting it according to scientific laws of form and colour.

The Constructivists created a new world out of cones, spheres, cubes and cylinders, according to Cézanne's precepts, but they practically confined themselves to the primary colours, red, blue, and yellow. This was an intellectual principle with them in which reason was the controlling element, though it dominated them less than the Cubists.

A liking for clearly defined forms and ingenious structures explained the Constructivists' passion for the products of technics, tools, and machines. They brought to art a fresh conception of beauty – the poetry of machines as an expression of modern civilisation. In its mania for objectivity and despite its social values, Constructivism, like Cubist analysis, necessarily developed into a form of intellectual non-representational art. Only Fernand Léger kept faith with its principles throughout his career, despite certain changes in his style.

Suprematism, exemplified by Malevitch, was a movement rising out of Constructivism, but still more austere in its insistence on reason and science. It could be described as a mystical code of line and colour. Little concerned with questions of space and matter, but impelled with a fierce desire for intellectual clarity, the Suprematists naturally attained the barest and most generalised form of abstract art, in which the subject became no more than a disembodied symbol.

Verism, Magic realism, Constructivism, and Suprematism, though they have ceased to exist as clearly defined movements, still exercise an influence on present trends in art, from Surrealism to non-representational art, not to mention some forms of Socialist realism as practised outside Soviet Russia.

As for Expressionism proper, after several years' neglect, it has achieved an astonishing return to favour, especially in Anglo-Saxon countries, in Central America, and among young nations such as Yugo-Slavia, Turkey, Israel, Czecho-Slovakia, etc.

Metaphysical art

Historians of art have given the name of 'metaphysical' to the invention of one man, Giorgio de Chirico, who was soon followed by three other Italians, two of them ex-Futurists – Carra, Morandi, Severini – and some lesser figures.

This form of painting, which showed, at the beginning, a resemblance to some of Boecklin's works, reached its peak between 1910 and 1917, though it has survived long after being renounced by its own creator.

Chirico developed a completely fantastic style by bringing a poetry composed of desolation, anguish and nightmare, into his landscapes and views of towns, his paintings of interiors and still life. In a flash of illumination he lays bare the strangeness and brooding solitude of certain empty corners in Italy, transformed into a prophetic vision. He transfers them to another world, where they are obliquely lit by the rays of some hidden sun. Blind statues and those mysterious muses who inspired the ancient heroes, changed into composite figures more like pieces of scaffolding than constructions, wander through the uncertain perspectives of his interiors or across his disturbing landscapes. Here and there in these compositions, which almost resemble the dream of a mad mathematician, the artist shocks the eye by deceptively painting some commonplace object.

Chirico's followers widened the range of his images and discoveries, without ever achieving his mysterious poetry, his skilful technique, his brilliance of colour. In the end his message can only be accepted as a striking revelation, unique in its kind – and it could be said to have had no repercussions, if it were not for the fact

Carlo Carra, 1911.   50

Giorgio de Chirico, 1917. 62

aul Klee, 1920.   150

Max Ernst, 19.

that metaphysical painting later found a place in the Surrealist revolution, of which it was undoubtedly a forerunner.

Since the time of Hieronymus Bosch or Archimboldo, the art of fantasy has never produced paintings which, in Chirico's own words, have so wholly 'transcended human limitations'.

Dada and Surrealism

Dadaism arose in 1917–18 out of an immense disgust for the war. A whole generation had come to the conclusion that nothing was of any importance. Some young men, particularly those who were most sensitive and who had suffered most, hardened their hearts and embarked together on the Dada movement. Its aim was to make a clean sweep; its methods were confusion and destruction. It proclaimed that everything, especially art, was nonsense. The inspiration of this trend towards anarchism and nihilism was found in the writings of Lautréamont, Mallarmé, Jacques Vaché, and Apollinaire, in some *collages* of Picasso, Braque, and the German Verists, and in the paintings of Chirico. It broke out at the same time in France, Switzerland, the United States and Germany; in Zurich it was organized by Tristan Tzara and Arp, in New York by Marcel Duchamp, and in Paris by André Breton and his friends Soupault and Eluard.

From 1919 Paris became the chief centre from which the Dadaists conducted a fierce campaign against morals, philosophy, religion, society, and all those 'false values' which, they declared, restricted the freedom of mankind. The same sort of freedom that was being claimed for words in poetry was claimed for images in painting. Beauty was a matter of chance, even a creation of chance. The artist had always to try to be at odds with everything, including himself, in case he should give way to his own taste.

Some time before the 1914 war Marcel Duchamp, who had been one of the French Cubists, had produced paintings, *collages*, and other work which were genuinely Dada in their rejection of artistic and scientific ideals. His works were an odd mixture, partly organic, partly mechanical, utterly free in construction and line, either dynamic in the Futurist or static in the Cubist style, and they had the unexpected charm of a lucky throw, a happy inspiration.

Kurt Schwitters, Max Ernst, Picabia, Man Ray, Hans Arp, and André Masson show different facets – and differences, whatever was claimed, of personal discipline – of this movement, which was necessarily self-destructive. It never reached its high water mark, but nevertheless it was the Dadaists who boldly prepared the way for Surrealism, which had genuinely positive aims.

To Surrealism fell the task of filling the gap left by Dada and exploring those irrational regions of the mind which Apollinaire had already called 'Surrealist', using every means, accepting science no less than intuition. The Surrealist Manifesto, drawn up by André Breton and signed by a small group of friends such as Eluard and Aragon, declared war on all those laws and conventions which stifled the human spirit. Liberation could only be achieved by rejecting reality, abandoning reason and all moral, religious, or aesthetic considerations, in order to surrender unreservedly to the infinite mystery of dreams and imagination. Imagination itself could build a 'real world' controlled by Baudelaire's 'logic of nonsense'. Dreams solved all problems because they clearly revealed the mind's authentic activity. Disciples of Freud, the Surrealists regarded themselves as 'recording apparatus' for the voice of the unconscious. They had a limitless belief in all the products of automatism.

Unlike Dada, which was fundamentally anarchical, Surrealism believed in organized collective action which would either establish its own revolution or link it with one already in existence – 'provided that it went far enough'. The political side came to nothing, several of its members deserting either to the conservative Right or to the orthodox Left, so that after 1930 the Surrealists confined their experiments to poetry and science, painting and the cinema.

It cannot be denied that the Surrealist movement has left a deep mark on painting in the latter half of the past fifty years. Max Ernst, Hans Arp, Paul Klee, Joan Miro, Picasso, Yves Tanguy, René Magritte, not to mention a number of younger names, have produced or are still producing some of the most striking works in this age. Surrealism differs from some other modern movements in not being bound to any technical theory of painting. It is in the very nature of its psychology that it has never laid down a style or technique of painting. Despite their undoubted mastery, the Surrealists have never practised art for art's sake. Subject matter has bulked larger than technique and, even if there is a psychological unity in all

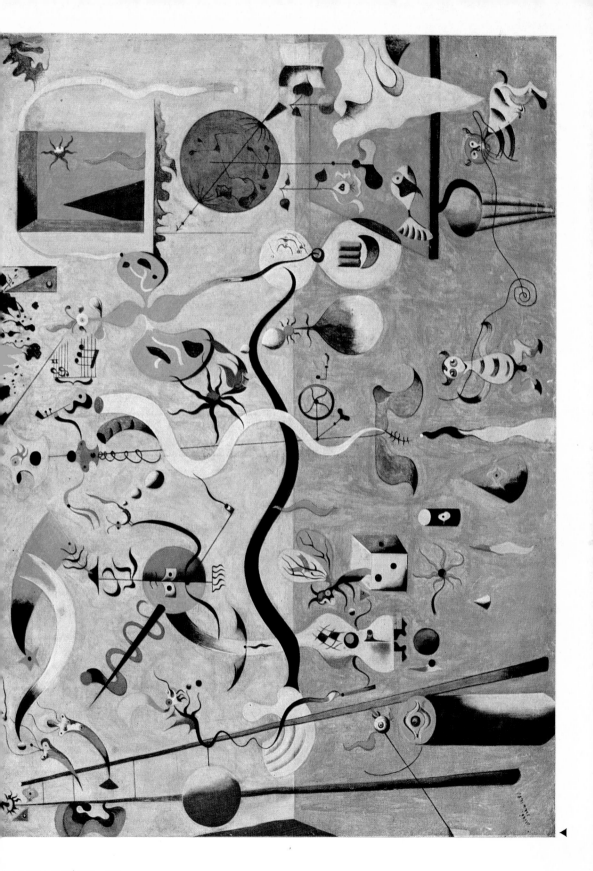

Joan Miro, 1924/1925. 215

44

Salvador Dali, 1936.

their work, the 'styles' of Klee, Miro, Arp, Ernst, and Magritte, to name only the most important, are as different as those of their distant forerunners, Bosch, Baldung, Goya, Ensor and Redon. That is why Surrealism can at one and the same time reveal to different critics romantic, reflective, Expressionist and abstract aspects – not to mention Salvador Dali's paranoïc hallucinations, which are definitely baroque.

Stripped of its party politics and its orthodox assertions, Surrealism has exercised an increasing influence on a gifted younger generation which, unsettled by the Second World War and obsessed with the problems of the atomic age, has tried to escape into satire and fantasy (Dubuffet), the nuclear spirals of a disrupted universe (Matta), the primitive mysticism of African and Caribbean rites (Wifredo Lam), a version of non-representational symbolism (Wols), or a return to Magic realism (Graves).

Naive Painting

It has been shown how the Cubists, in the years 1907–1909, found their inspiration in negro sculpture and how the first Expressionists sought theirs in the idols and enchantments of the South Seas. The Surrealists' search for the exotic made them probe deeper. Not content with the art treasures of primitive peoples, they went straight back to the most genuine and direct origin of artistic creation – the art of children and madmen, and Naive painting. It is one of Surrealism's claims to fame that it discovered Naive painting and revealed its importance, to the great enrichment of modern sensibility. Apollinaire and Picasso, by bringing to light the genius of the Douanier Rousseau, the age's most delicate master of colour, had already opened people's eyes to this art before 1914. A proper respect for the art of ordinary men who are yet 'not quite like other men' has succeeded the scornful laughter of earlier days. It is true that every Sunday painter is not 'a master of popular art', but the genuine Naives are always true poets and authentic artists. Self-educated and comparatively uncultured, they never produce work which is simply an inferior copy of 'great' or traditional art. The Naive painter has no academic background, but he is neither a failure nor a bungler; he starts from scratch, acknowledging no master. In his own view he is a realist, getting up his subject and studying nature, but a dream-like quality and his own instinct transfigure his forms and control his work. A deliberate line, a strong outline without any projecting shadows, a clear horizon, a succession of vistas, a multitude of details, and above all a harmony of colour which never errs, these mark the work of most Naive painters. Yet each has his own style which can be recognised easily enough. In general their preference goes to landscapes, portraits, and scenes of daily life, but some Naive painters produce an art of pure fantasy which often shows childishly erotic traits.

Men of the people, workers, porters, housewives, labourers, barrow boys, they paint only for themselves, impelled by their own need and making no other claim. This homely art for homely people has ended by finding its way into our galleries and into our minds no less than the work of acknowledged masters, simply through its own plastic merits.

Socialist Realism

The masters of popular art, or Naive painters, are perhaps the only artists who, bound to the people, produce an art which, of its nature, is for the people. They are the individualists of popular traditional art, which is really an expression of the whole community. Yet there is a theory more or less freely shared by hundreds of artists throughout the world according to which art should serve an ideology which, among other things, envisages the emancipation of the masses by culture. But this culture is conceived especially for the multitude and should be readily acceptable to the masses; it is very different from 'the anarchic, irresponsible, individualist, formalist, and decadent culture of civilisations which are alien and hostile'.

According to this theory, art should do battle on two fronts, against ignorance, indifference, and insensitiveness on one side, and on the other against every form of art which cannot be grasped by the proletariat, or is useless and even harmful

Raoul Dufy, 1929. 87

Fernand Léger, 1954.   177

Ben Nicholson, 1956.   239

to it. The chief aim of literature and the arts, according to this same theory, is to help the proletariat to realise its power and importance, to fulfil its destiny – and in this the arts find their complete, if not their only justification.

That is why Socialist realism, in its paintings and sculpture, no less than in its novels and motion pictures, confines itself to exalting the people and their country, their leaders, their revolutionary past, their victories, their achievements, and their faith in the future. Everything that fails to glorify the community is cast aside – nude studies, still life, and even more decidedly any preoccupation with pure form – just as every deviation is mercilessly condemned.

Although Socialist realism claims that it does not put forward any particular style and that it is as opposed to pessimistic naturalism as to conventional middle-class art, its artistic theories show some traces of pre-1914 realism, with a few traits of Luminism. Devotion to traditional craftsmanship goes hand in hand with a refusal to experiment in composition. The subject of a painting, in the sense of its 'story', dictates its form.

In the beginning, when the October revolution was far from having consolidated its gains and fighting artists were not yet under the ban of a dogmatic orthodoxy, Socialist realism showed very great promise of an original and monumental art (A. Deineka). This is the form – it might be called 'freely committed' – in which the movement achieved its finest flights, in Soviet Russia, in Mexico, France, and Italy, often among artists who were opposed to the government of their country and did not have to conform to any State orthodoxy.

The future will show whether the cause of Socialist realism has not been better and more effectively served by such heretics as Fernand Léger, Diego Rivera, Orozco, Siqueiros, Guttuso, Ben Shahn, not to mention Picasso, than by most of those who have confused a revolutionary 'subject' with a revolutionary 'attitude'. Meanwhile the enemies of State Socialist realism have been able to enjoy themselves by pointing out that, for all its generous aims, it has descended to the level of hypocrisy and sentimentality, optimism and easy symbolism associated with the worst type of academic art. This does not alter the fact that millions of people believe in it, without even suspecting what is the real plastic problem of our age.

The Independents

Before turning to Abstract art, which will conclude this preface, we must pay tribute to a few independent artists whose genius has left a deep imprint on the spirit and development of modern art. Although their work can frequently be assimilated to one or other of the great artistic movements of the period, the artists in question are often fierce individualists, self-taught men, rootless exiles, recluses, wanderers who do not easily conform to a team-spirit and remain on the fringe of the group with which they show the most affinity.

Thus, Utrillo and Modigliani, though intimately associated with the glorious adventure of the Ecole de Paris, managed to keep their own personalities intact and eventually made their mark with a purely poetic art, in opposition to the systematic styles of their period. The first, Utrillo, son of Suzanne Valadon and adopted son of the whole Bohemian population of Montmartre, took care to remain outside the movements which were beyond his powers; aware of the qualities and limitations of his gifts, he deliberately confined himself to a naïvely refined type of painting, scientifically ingenuous, using a bold, sparkling palette from which stand out whites and greys of an unusual delicacy. His best period coincided with the height of Fauvism, between 1908 and 1910.

Amedeo Modigliani, a Tuscan, also received the full onslaught of the masters of the moment from the date of his arrival in Paris (1906) onwards; but if he made any concessions to Lautrec, Picasso and Brancusi, they were only small. A hyper-sensitive artist, bred on the fine traditions of the Quattrocento, gifted both as a sculptor and as a painter, he created a style of his own, a style both lyrical and moving, and always profoundly human. None surpassed him in absorbing and sublimating the influence of Negro sculpture, especially that of the Gaboon which corresponded so perfectly with his own temperament. Graphically his art approaches Fauvism and Expressionism, but his drawing is subtler, as is his colour, which is composed of broken tone-values. He might be called the Botticelli of modern times.

Soutine, on the other hand, is all violence, all nervous energy. Self-taught, mal-adjusted to the end of his life, he carried his Jewish nostalgia and anxiety with him through Germany and France, embodying the exaggerated images of his over-acute vision in a bitter, ardent, instinctive style. A ruthless observer, powerful

Alfred Manessier, 1956. 190

Afro, 1953. 2

56   Willem de Kooning, 1955.

colorist and tormented soul, he created some of the most horrifyingly expressionistic pictures of the century. In Soutine's work there is something of Kokoschka,
but a Kokoschka in a perpetual fever.

Kokoschka himself, a true nomad although he was trained in Vienna and Berlin,
has a special place in German Expressionism, at first as a pioneer, later as a creator.
A visionary, obsessed with ethical and spiritual problems, he gives free rein to his
bizarre intuition in portraits, groups and landscapes painted in flashing colour
furrowed by biting drawing. His are amongst the most poignant portraits of the
century. No other Expressionist has equalled the dramatic fire or epic drive of
Kokoschka.

Although an integral part of the Ecole de Paris, Marc Chagall is nevertheless the
great outsider in French painting. Everything about him separates him from the
formal movements of the day. His melancholy temperament and child-like imagination remained constantly faithful to his ghetto in Witebsk, his people, his
troubles, his joys, his hopes and above all his religion. He derives from no one;
his spontaneous drawing, brilliant palette, mischievous wit and bizarre fantasy
belong to him and him alone. On the other hand, the Expressionist movement
owes much to him. In the intensity of his colour and the daring of his transpositions, he rivals Matisse. A man of feeling as well as a poet of immense
charm, Chagall is unique as a painter of modern fairy-tales.

The fact that Georges Rouault is considered the only French Expressionist is
enough to single him out as one of the strong points of the art of today. Both the
rough, satirical, dark works of his early years (swollen prostitutes, formless law-
yers and judges, sad clowns) and the religious compositions of his last thirty years
reveal him as a powerful artist, serious, generous, noble, with a certain mysticism,
an acute sense of the 'human condition' and a religious ideal as sincere as it is
lofty. By breaking with all the disciplines of art he succeeded in giving his colours
a clarion brightness, while reserving for black a key position in the constructural
and pictural scheme.

Many other contemporary artists deserve the name of 'independent', but since
most of them are also in the front ranks of important groups, they have been
dealt with in other sections.

Non-Representational Art

Although the phrase 'Abstract art' is as inaccurate as Fauvism, Cubism, Pointillism, and other journalistic terms, it has become generally accepted to cover a wide range of clearly defined works, principles, and ideas, despite differences of opinion inside the movement.

Broadly speaking it refers to works of art in which the representational element has either been so treated as to be unrecognisable, or deliberately avoided – the painting having been conceived without any thought of representing a material impression. In the same very general way it is possible to distinguish between the abstract art which has done away with representation – a step taken by some Cubists and more recently by Ben Nicholson, Vieira da Silva, and Nicolas de Staël – and the abstract art whose original inspiration is to rise above it – as in the case of Mondrian, Kandinsky, Malevitch, etc. These two attitudes cannot be classed together, for the first is an art deliberately opposed to nature, the second simply ignores it.

Contrary to a widely held opinion, Abstract art is by no means a post-war phenomenon. Although it has been introduced into some countries since 1945 and has come to the fore more recently, its beginnings go back to the great days before 1914. The first purely abstract paintings were made by Kandinsky in 1910, by Malevitch in 1913, and by Mondrian in 1914. It has moreover been shown above that most of the leading movements in the past fifty years – apart from Surrealism, Socialist realism, and Magic realism – carried within them seeds from which non-representational art was bound to develop. The reason for this is that at the beginning of everything there always appears the figure of Cézanne, the pioneer to whom is due the 'purification' of forms, colours, and ideas.

The movent against naturalism with which the century began was bound to lead to a rejection of representational elements, once its principles were carried to their natural conclusion, not only because they had already been simplified by the Cubists, Constructivists, Orphists etc., but because each of these movements had a left wing which ignored the intervening phase and went straight towards a complete breaking down of the object envisaged – Kandinsky and Marc among the *Blaue Reiter* group, Picasso in the crisis of Cubism and Mondrian when he left the Cubists, Severini among the Futurists and Léger among the Constructivists,

Ivan Generalic, 1934.

not to mention such Surrealists as Klee and Miro. Finally there were trends which could be summed up by a single leading figure – Mondrian's Neo-Plasticism, Malevitch's Suprematism, and Delaunay's Orphism.

Modern art is constantly swinging between two poles, rule and instinct, reflection and exclamation, reason and fantasy. It would be tempting to think that Abstract art is naturally attracted towards the pole of intellectual discipline, with its rules and its attachment to order, harmony, and geometry. For a long time this was indeed the fact, and many of the finest non-representational works arose from this great need for an intellectual equilibrium in a world of chaos. Most of the gradations within non-representational art could be grouped between the austere Mondrian and the intuitive Delaunay, inasmuch as reason controls and orders their work – Herbin, Magnelli, Servranckx, Nicholson, Kupka, Moholy-Nagy, Mortensen, Adam, Vasarely, etc.

Yet it has been shown above that Expressionism too gave rise to an Abstract art which, unlike the static non-representational art based on reason, was chiefly concerned with dynamic expression (Kandinsky and Klee). This type of art is wholly based on lyrical and dramatic feeling, and its only appeal is to intuition. Its aim is to summon up psychological moods, and its exponents have a belief in the psychological meaning of line and colour. Their only 'rule' is a balance of contradictory feelings which are constantly fresh and changing. Their original inspiration being deeper and more unconscious, their line and colour are more disturbing, owing much to automatic and symbolic impulses beyond their control, mysterious perhaps even to the artist himself. This art of embodying psychological states without making use of representation – that is to say recognisable forms – separates the Abstract Expressionists from the Surrealists.

The Surrealists give an objective form to their fantastic dreams by using images which are perfectly comprehensible, but absurd in their context; each individual intensifies his own imagination. Abstract Expressionism is far more deeply rooted in the psychology of mankind, and so unintentionally returns to the art of the remote ages of myth.

No other movement in modern art has followed its 'exotic' inspiration right back to the childhood of man. Sir Herbert Read has said that 'dream-thinking' represents the primitive phase of human culture before it has reached the age of reason. There is no need to emphasize the striking resemblance between some works of Kandinsky, Klee, Miro, Masson, Arp, and the ritual paintings of prehistoric and primitive peoples; this is no casual likeness, but a psychological and artistic fact which can be scientifically proved. Far from making a break with the past, Abstract art has expressed it in its truest and purest form. Far from being a symptom of decline, it represents a fresh beginning.

The wide influence of Chinese and Japanese ideograms, which are perfect examples of myth and symbol, on a number of non-representational artists – Tobey, Kline, Soulages, and all the modern school of Japan – confirms this link between Abstract art and the oldest of human cultures.

Despite the universal nature of its style, Abstract Expressionism, especially in the last fifteen years, has adopted a great variety of forms in accord with the character of the individual artist. Characters and colourists as different as Bazaine and Sam Francis, Hitchens and Capogrossi, Jorn and Appel, Hartung and Winter, Wols and Riopelle, Corneille and Pollock, Lubarda and Afro, Baumeister and Poliakoff, Manessier and Werner, Nay and Santomaso, Masson and De Kooning, have brilliantly practised an art which opens up a new world, the world of psychological space.

Only to list these painters and their very varied styles is to show that this form of art is still evolving and still holds immense possibilities. The recent triumphs of such Abstract painters as the Tachists, Action painters, and others have greatly widened the scope for experiment. Yet great though these possibilities are, they are not inexhaustible, and there are already signs of a new academic orthodoxy arising. In general, the imitators are talented rather than genuinely inspired.

Conclusion

Nobody can claim to prophesy how art will evolve in the future. It would be absurd to attempt even a very general estimate, at the date of this book's publication. The rising generation will attend to that and will quite probably emphasize facts which hardly seem important to us at the moment, for it is always possible that values will change.

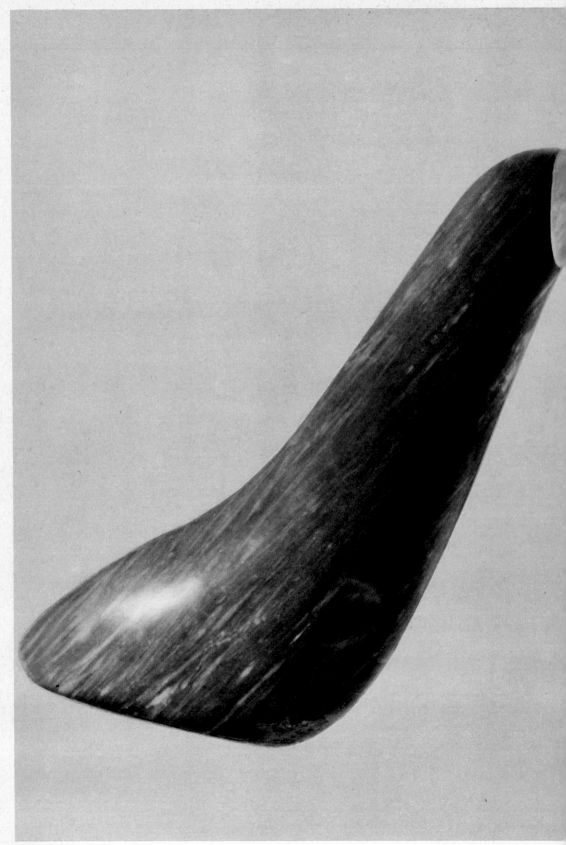

Constantin Brancusi, 1943.

Jacques Lipchitz, 1923/1925.

Julio Gonzalez, 1937.   111

Antoine Pevsner, 1950/1951. 2

Marino Marini, 1953/1954.

Yet one conclusion can scarcely be avoided: art today, as in the past fifty years, still shows two main trends, one speculative and intellectual, the other emotional and instinctive. Representational and abstract painting and sculpture has resulted from both these tendencies. The real division in art today is not between the concrete and the abstract, but between firstly the search for a transcendental equilibrium based on reason, and secondly the rejection of this equilibrium in favour of a greater freedom in expressing emotion.

Looked at from this point of view – and from this point in time – Cubism, Neo-Plasticism, Orphism, Suprematism, Magic realism, and all geometric abstract art are grouped on one side, while on the other side stand Fauvism, Futurism, Expressionism, Surrealism, and three-quarters of non-representational art – all no more than variations of a single outlook. Yet both these trends can show artists who accept some form of discipline or who demand some degree of freedom, with the result that the dividing line between them is constantly being blurred, and both are seen as aspects of one complex phenomenon – the solution to the 20th century's plastic problem, either by facing the present or by anticipating the future. The artist today is both a witness and a prophet.

There is a surprising resemblance between this and a moral code accepted equally by believers and freethinkers, who each apply it in their own way. Yet there are some important figures such as Picasso, Chagall, Klee, and several 'independents' who make free use of a number of styles at once and so achieve a synthesis which proves that there is no insurmountable barrier between them.

Sculpture too can claim several of these synthetic artists such as Brancusi, a great artist in his own right, Gonzalez, Laurens, Zadkine, and Moore. Among the triumphs of modern art, sculpture, which evolves slowly and remains consistent, offers a more clear-cut, overall picture than painting. With their more restricted means, which leave no margin for error, such men as Lehmbruck, Barlach, Arp, Lipchitz, Pevsner, Gabo, Calder, Marini, Gargallo, Giacometti, Martini, not to mention younger names, have followed up the various achievements of modern painting which they have developed and often surpassed. Although less spectacular, the part played by sculpture has been no less important than that played by painting, both in working out the problems of Abstract art and in its contribution to Cubism, Expressionism, and Surrealism.

Especially in recent years sculptors have introduced new, interesting and attractive forms which may well foreshadow future aspects of art. Certainly more and more sculpture is being produced which turns abstract elements, rough forms, and miscellaneous fragments into genuine 'beings' – in the sense that they are conceived, put together, and inspired in accord with the laws of biology. These creatures which the naturalist might call 'monsters' draw their life from a world in process of formation, where the various orders of nature are still interconnected. No less than the painters, such sculptors as Roszak, Zadkine, Moore, Chadwick, Mirko, Uhlmann, and others uncover laws of life and matter whose existence had not been suspected before, so bearing witness to the deep realism of modern art, which has explored reality in its remotest corners – the organic structure of things. It is to be noted that many Expressionist sculptors, such as Marini, Lipchitz, Wotruba, and Armitage, while they practise representational art, share the aims of Abstract art in their determination to seize on the essential aspects of life. It has moreover been proved that some geometric and abstract sculpture, the work of Pevsner, Gabo, Hepworth, and others, is in perfect agreement with figures used by contemporary mathematicians to express complicated algebraic formulas. Once again the modern artist, using only his intuition, has shown his insight into the mysteries of the universe.

This brief summary may be brought to an end by recalling the startling revelations made by modern art in the realms of psychology and in the disturbing mysteries of the subconscious, a final proof that the art of mankind has never achieved such complete and responsible control of the universe, with all its implications of anguish and ecstasy, pride and despair.

Modern art, growing out of Cézanne's three little apples, has made an heroic effort to adapt purely plastic means to an investigation of the present and the past, the visible and the invisible, reality and fantasy, sense and nonsense, matter and spirit, the depths and the heights.

But it must be said, in the words of Picasso, that modern art is 'not a search, but a creation'. It has produced a spirited reflection of our age and behaviour, entirely our own, to sadden or rejoice us. Modern art will go down to posterity as an image of the past fifty years with its failures and its triumphs. In the phrase of André Malraux, it will be remembered not as a passing fashion, but as a period.

Emile Langui

Where a colour picture has had to be turned sideways to obtain the maximum size of reproduction, an arrowhead (Δ) indicates the bottom edge of the picture.

Georges Seurat, 1888.

Claude Monet, 1919.

Vincent van Gogh, 1888.

Vincent van Gogh, 1888.

James Ensor, 1889.

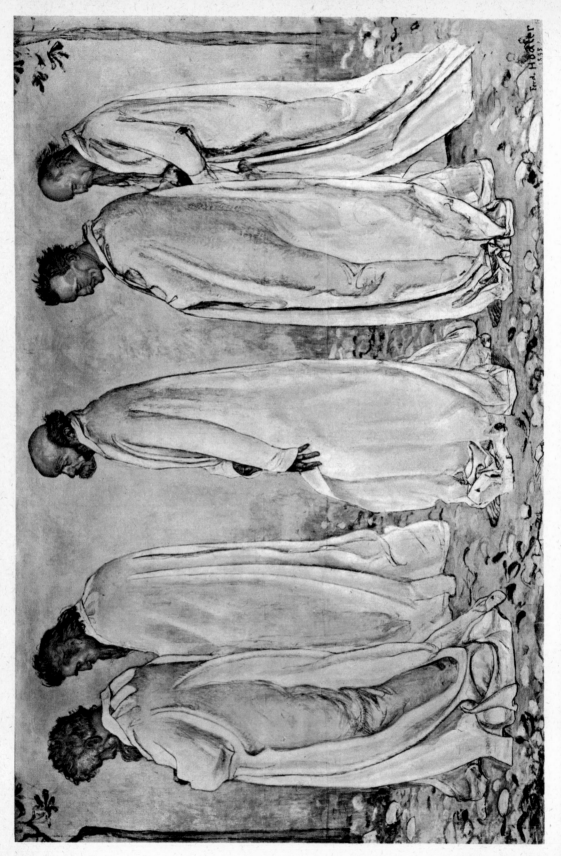

Ferdinand Hodler, 1895.   132

Paul Gauguin, 1896.

Henri Rousseau, 1890.

Paul Cézanne, 1904.

Paul Cézanne, c. 1875.   54

ard Vuillard, 1899.   328

Walter Richard Sickert, 1914.   292

Pierre Bonnard, 1907.   28

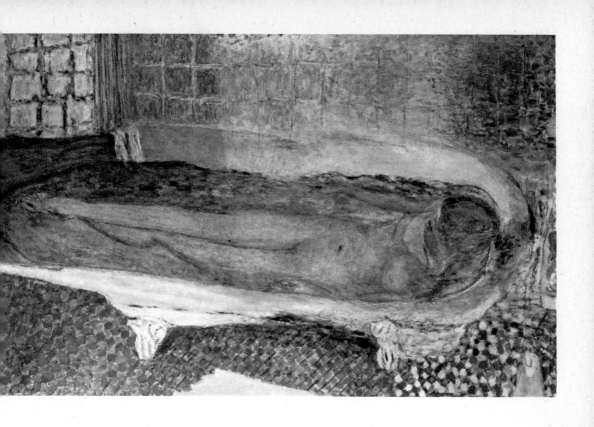

Pierre Bonnard. 30

Pierre Bonnard. 31

aurice Utrillo, c. 1908. 317

aurice Utrillo, 1915. 318

Helena Schjerfbeck, 1907. 277

Kai Fjell, 1937. 94

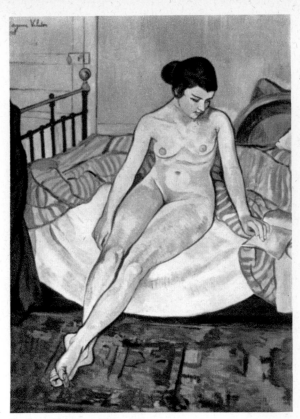

Suzanne Valadon, 1922.   319

eodor Csontvary, 1907.   66

Maurice de Vlaminck, 1907.

Lovis Corinth, 1921.   64

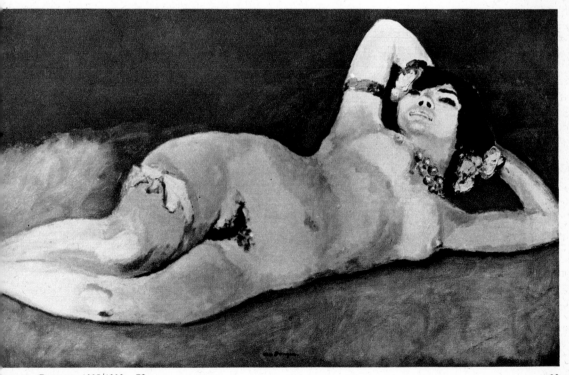

Georges Braque, 1906.

Raoul Dufy, 1914. 85

Raoul Dufy, 1906. 84

Albert Marquet, 1904. 200

Henri Matisse, 1913. 209

Henri Matisse, 1911. 206

Henri Matisse, 1917. 210

Henri Matisse, 1911.

Henri Matisse, c. 1910.   205

Henri Matisse, 1910.   208

Rik Wouters, 1912.   333

Pablo Picasso, 1908. 251

Pablo Picasso, 1908.   252

Pablo Picasso, 1909/1910. 2

Juan Gris, 1925.   117

Louis Marcoussis, 1936.

Frantisek Kupka, 1913.   167

Noël Roger de La Fresnaye, 1913.   169

Noël Roger de La Fresnaye, 1914.

Georges Braque, 1956.   42

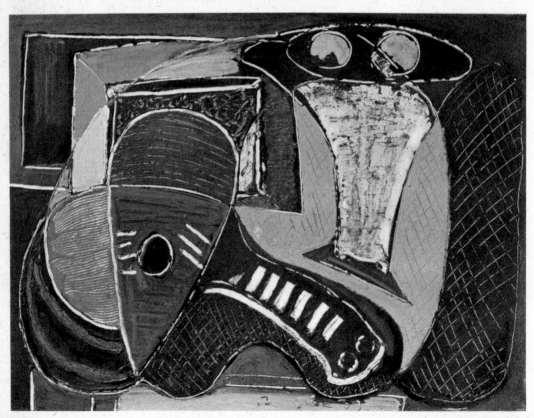

Emil Filla, 1933.   93

Georges Braque, 1925.　39

André Derain, 1913. 74

Paula Modersohn-Becker, 1906. 219

Wassily Kandinsky, 1909. 140

Wassily Kandinsky, 1910.

Franz Marc, 1914. 1█

Franz Marc, 1913. 1█

Emil Nolde, 1912. 241

Ernst Ludwig Kirchner, 1907.   146

Christian Rohlfs, 1913.   268

Ernst Ludwig Kirchner, 1913.

la tour 1910   r delaunay 1910

Nathalie Gontcharova, 1910. 110

Robert Delaunay, 1912/1913. 71

Jacques Villon, 1949.   323

ques Villon, 1953.   324

Lyonel Feininger, 1913.

John Marin, 1922. 196

John Marin, 1926. 197

Umberto Boccioni, 1911.

Umberto Boccioni, 1913. 25

Gino Severini, 1912. 290

LE PASSAGE de la vierge à la mariée   MARCEL DUCHAMP 12

Marcel Duchamp, 1912.

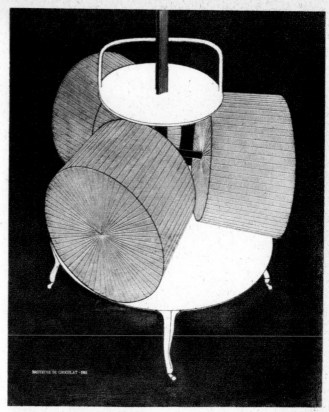

Marcel Duchamp, 1914. 81

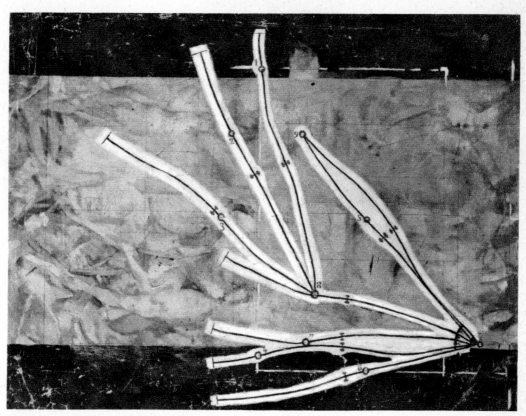

Marcel Duchamp, 1914. 82

LA NUIT ESPAGNOLE

Sangre Andaluza

FRANCIS PICABIA

Francis Picabia, 1912.

Giorgio de Chirico, 1914

Giorgio de Chirico, 1912. 60

Carlo Carra, 1917. 51

Giorgio Morandi, 1918.   230

Giorgio Morandi, 1957.   231

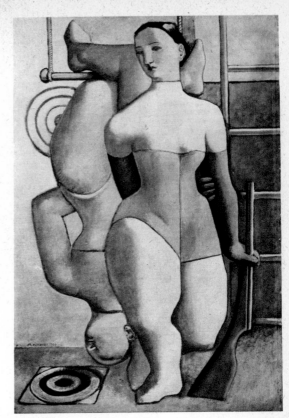

Massimo Campigli, 1926. 48

ilippo de Pisis, 1937. 258

Mario Sironi, 1947. 294

Kurt Schwitters, 1920. 282

Kurt Schwitters, c. 1919.   281

Kurt Schwitters, 1925.   283

Paul Klee, 1914.   149

Paul Klee, 1923.   152

Paul Klee, 1923.   151

Paul Klee, 1937.   154

Paul Klee, 1938.   155

Paul Klee, 1939.   157

Paul Klee, 1939.   156

Paul Klee, 1929.

Schiele, 1917. 276

Amedeo Modigliani. 221

Picasso, 1923. 254

Georges Rouault, 1930/1939. 271

rges Rouault, 1935.   272

Marcel Gromaire, 1925.   118

Chaïm Soutine, 1920. 299

skar Kokoschka, 1909. 159

kar Kokoschka, 1919. 161

Karl Schmidt-Rottluff, 1913.

Karl Schmidt-Rottluff, 1921. 280

Erich Heckel, 1916. 125

Emil Nolde, 1933. 242

Otto Mueller, 1927. 234

Ernst Ludwig Kirchner, 1917. 148

Oskar Kokoschka, 1927. 162

Georges Grosz, 1917/1918. 11

Oskar Schlemmer, 1930.   278

Carl Hofer, 1933. 133

Max Beckmann, 1930.   17

Sluyters, 1917.   295

Constant Permeke, 1929. 246

Constant Permeke, 1935. 247

Jean Brusselmans, 1939.   44

Cevat Dereli, 1956.   75

ts van den Berghe, 1929. 20

Joseph Kutter, 1930.   168

Herman Kruijder, 1933.   165

Scipione, 1929/1930. 284

Vaclav Spala, 1929. 301

Pablo Picasso, 1941.   2

Rufino Tamayo, 1950. 305

Graham Sutherland, 1946.   303

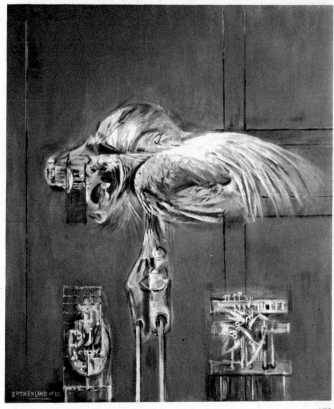

Graham Sutherland, 1955.   304

Paul Nash, 1945.

Ivon Hitchens, 1956.

essai Tomioka, 1908. 310

Ryuzaburo Umehara, 1952. 316

Marc Chagall, 1913. 58

rc Chagall, 1956.   59

Mordechai Ardon, 1954.   6

Max Ernst, 1939. 91

Joan Miro, 1934.

an Miro, 1926.   216

an Miro, 1953.   218

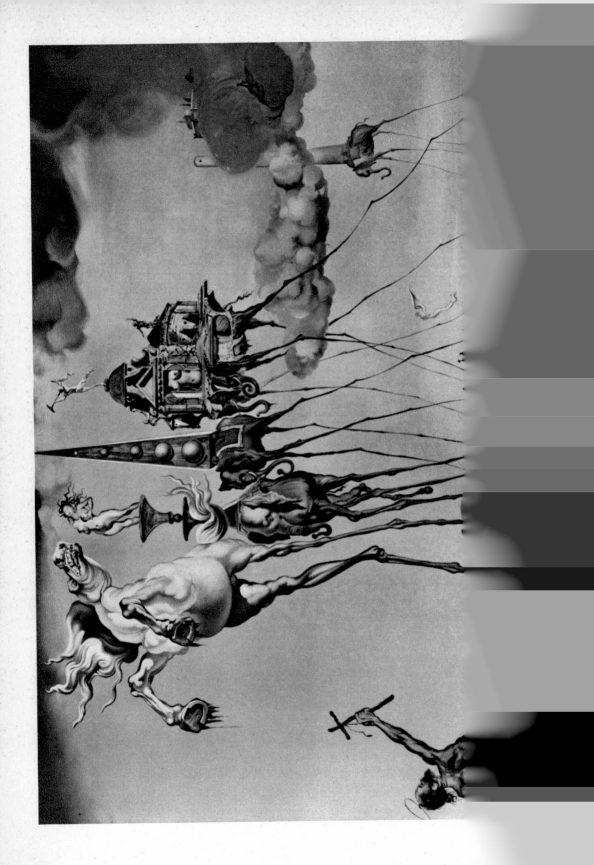

Yves Tanguy, 1954. 306

René Magritte, 1929.   186

Paul Delvaux, 1941.   72

Josef Sima, 1933. 293

Arshile Gorky, 1947. 113

Morris Hirshfield, 1945.   130

Séraphine, 1929.   286

Ivan Generalic, 1943. 102

Krsto Hegedusic, 1932. 126

Ben Shan, 1950.

Edgard Tytgat, 1923.   314

arley Toorop, 1932. 312

Nicolas Ghika, 1952. 103

Otto Dix, 1924.

Renato Guttuso, 1956. 122

Lewis Le Brocquy, 1951. 175

Diego Rivera, 1926. 266

José Clemente Orozco, 1920. 244

Candido Portinari, 1944. 261

José Gutierrez Solana: 297

Isidore Opsomer, 1942.   243

Edward Hopper, 1939.   134

Alexandre M. Guerassimov, 1956.   120

Brodsky, 1930.   43

Alexandre I. Laktionov, 1947. 171

Martiros Sarian, 1957. 275

Simeon Tchujkov, 1948. 307

Kukryniksy, 1947/1948. 166

Alexandre A. Deineka, 1928.

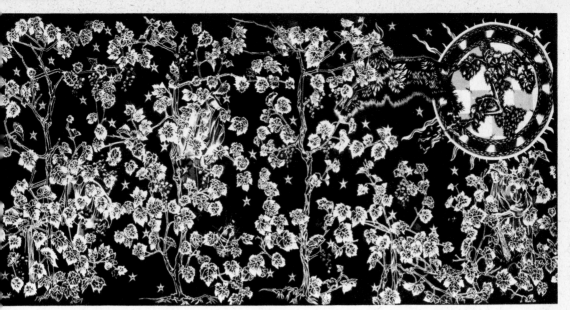

an Lurçat, 1956.   183

Henri-Georges Adam, 1949.   1

Wassily Kandinsky, 1912. 1

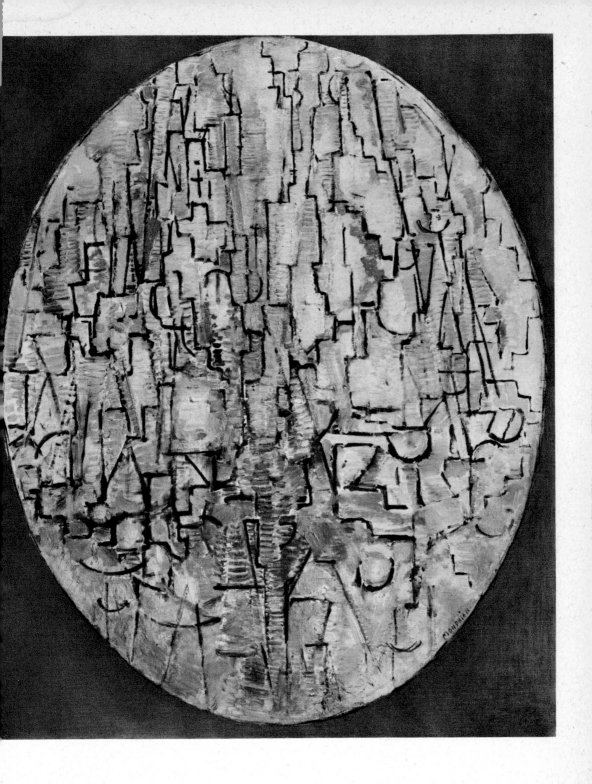

Piet Mondrian, 1921. 225

Kasimir Malevitch, p. 1915.   189

Willi Baumeister, 1923.   14

Victor Servranckx, 1923.   2

Làszlo Moholy-Nagy, 1939.   223

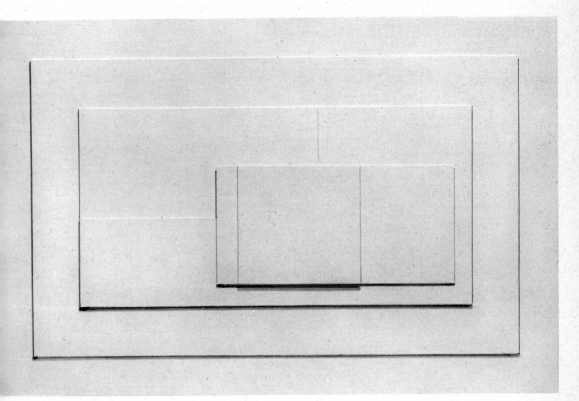

Alberto Magnelli, 1952.

Jean Bazaine, 1950. 16

Maria Elena Vieira da Silva, 1955. 322

Carlos Botelho, 1955. 32

Ernst Wilhelm Nay, 1957.

Theodor Werner, 1951.   329

Winter, 1951.   330

Renato Birolli, 1957.

Giuseppe Capogrossi, 1956.   49

Giuseppe Santomaso, 1953.   274

Marc Tobey, 1956.

Franz Kline, 1955. 158

ichi Inoue, 1957.   135

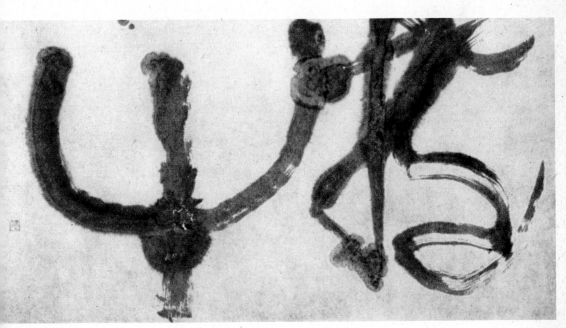

Richard Mortensen, 1955. 2

Pierre Soulages, 1958.   298

Nicolas de Staël, 1952.   302

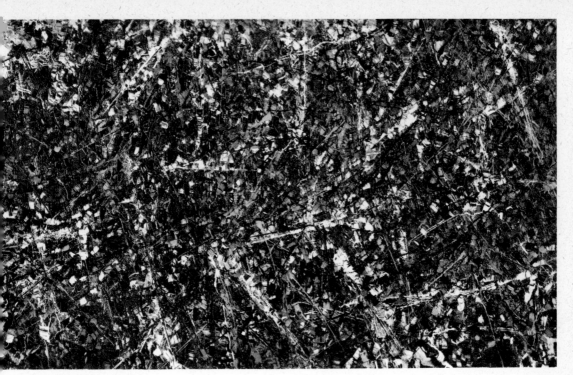

an-Paul Riopelle, 1952.   265

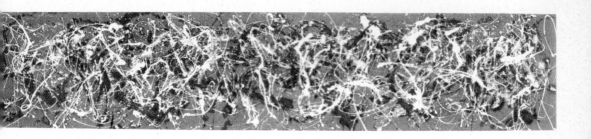

ckson Pollock, 1949.   260

Karel Appel, 1957.

Asger Jorn, 1956/1957. 1

Dubuffet, 1945.   79

Petar Lubarda, 1952. 182

Herbert Boeckl, 1957. 27

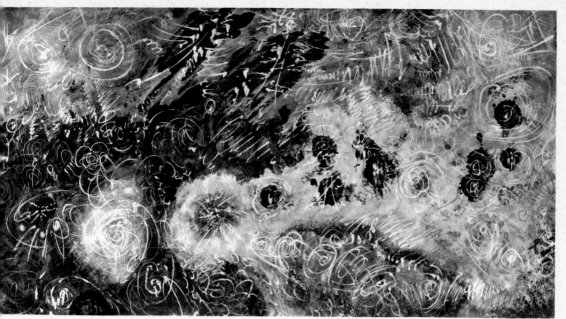

...dré Masson, 1956.   203

...is Graves, 1944.   114

Roberto Sebastiano Matta Echaùrren, 1955.

Sidney Nolan, 1955. 240

Krsto Hegedusic, 1956. 127

Georges Braque, 1956.

Charles Despiau, 1929. 76

Aristide Maillol, 1939/1943. 187

guste Renoir, 1915/1916. 263

George Minne, 1897.   212   Rik Wouters, 1913.

Ernst Barlach, 1923. 13

Alexandre Archipenko, 1920/1923. 5   Hermann Blumenthal, 1928. 23

Raymond Duchamp-Villon, 1914.

erto Boccioni, 1913. 26

Henri Laurens, 1938.

Pablo Gargallo. 98

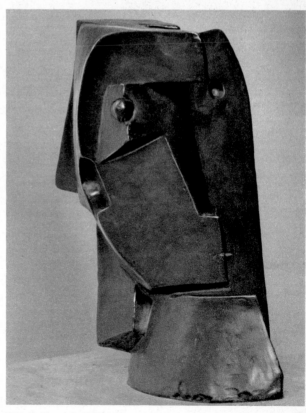

Otto Gutfreund. 1919. 121

Jacques Lipchitz, 1949/1957.

car Jespers, 1930/1931. 138

Julio Gonzalez, 1937.   112

Theodor Roszak, 1951. 2

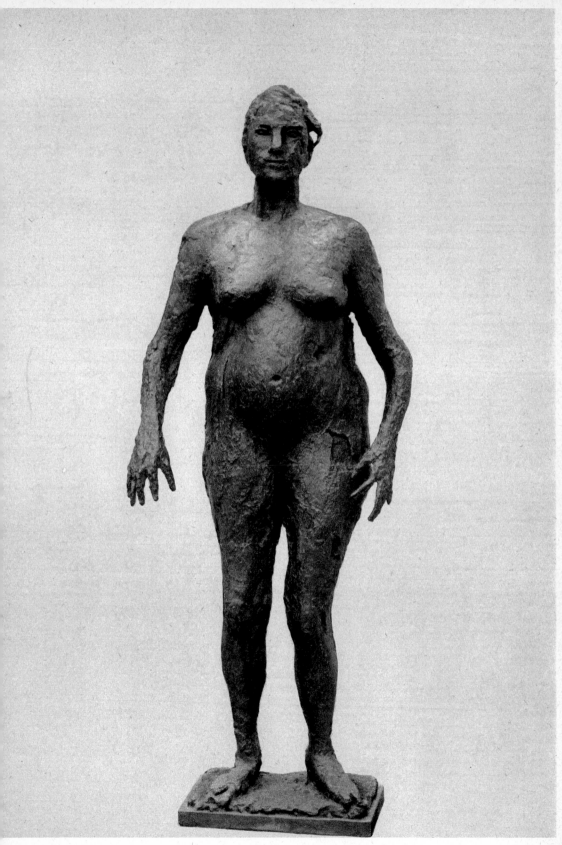

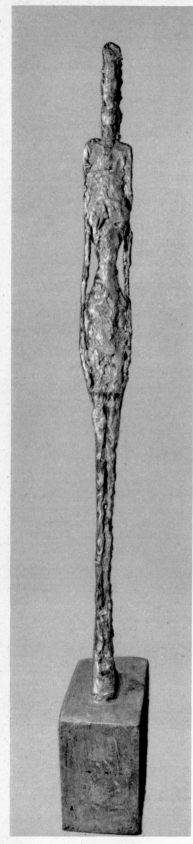

Alberto Giacometti, 1957.   105   Alberto Giacometti, 1935.   104

Fritz Wotruba, 1949.   332

ésostris César Vitullo, 1952.   325

Giacomo Manzu, 1955/1957. 1

Marcello Mascherini, 1952. 202

Marino Marini, 1940. 1

Arturo Martini, 1934. 2

ari Andriessen, 1951. 3

Emilio Greco, 1957. 115

　　　　　Nicolas V. Tomski, 1954.　311　　　　　　　　　　　　　Ivan D. Chadr, 1939.

rge T. Konenkov, 1933.   163

Gustav Seitz, 1952/1954.   285

gène V. Voutetich, 1955.   327

Alexandre P. Kibalnikov, 1956.   145

Constantin Brancusi, 1925. 35

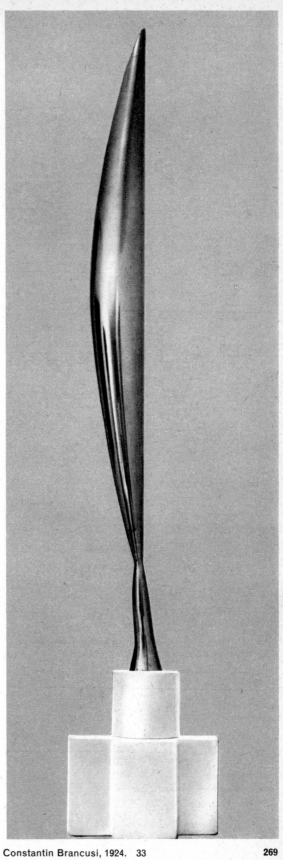

Constantin Brancusi, 1924.   33

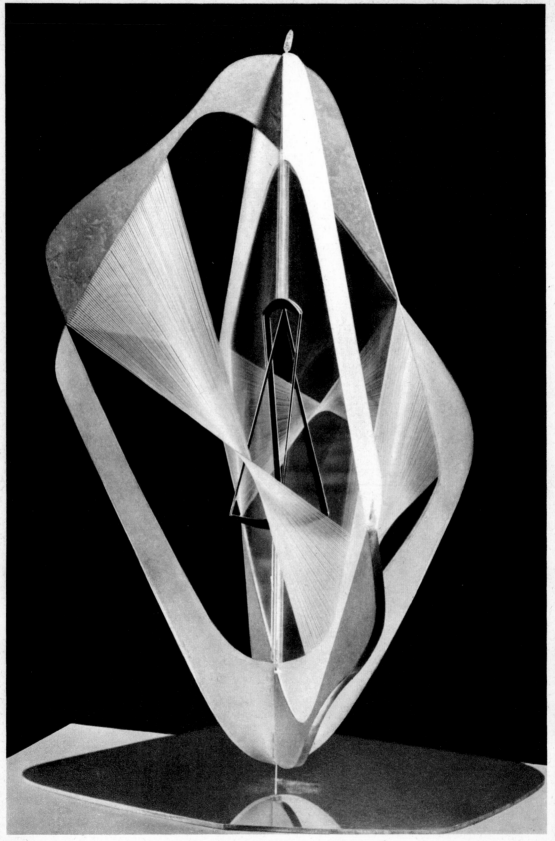

Naum Gabo, 1953. 97

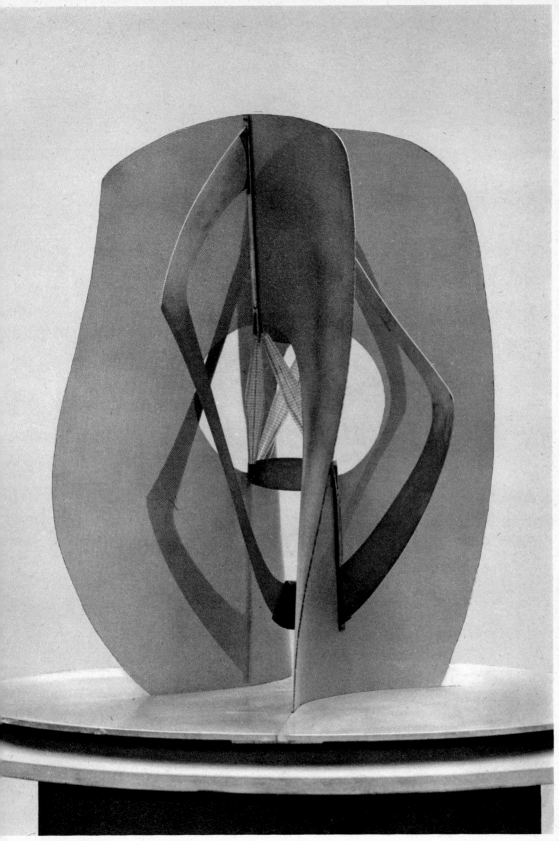

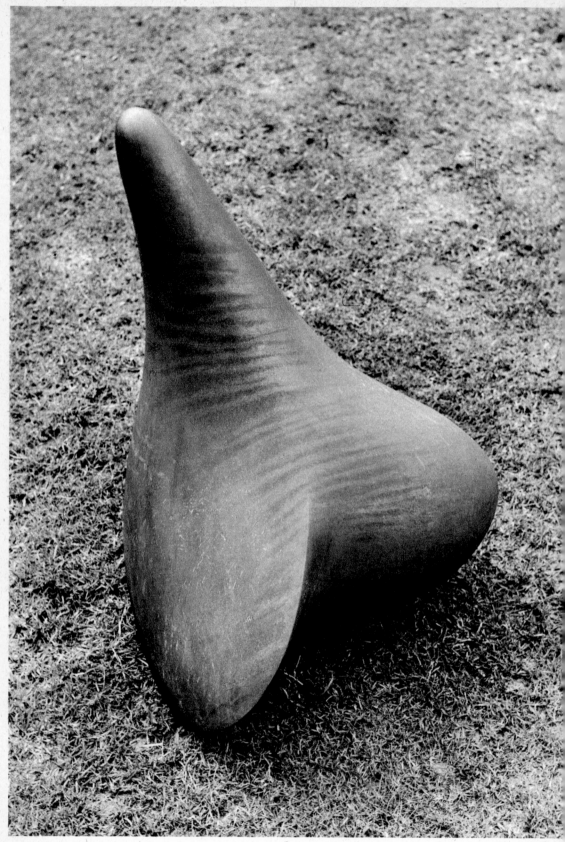

Hans Arp, 1935.

Barbara Hepworth, 1955.   129

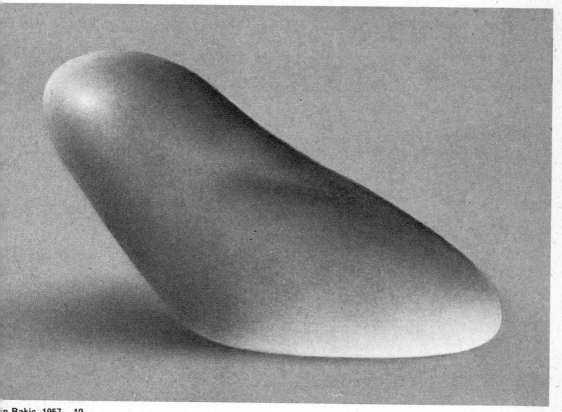

n Bakic, 1957.   12

Alexander Calder, 1958.

Robert Jacobsen, 1951.

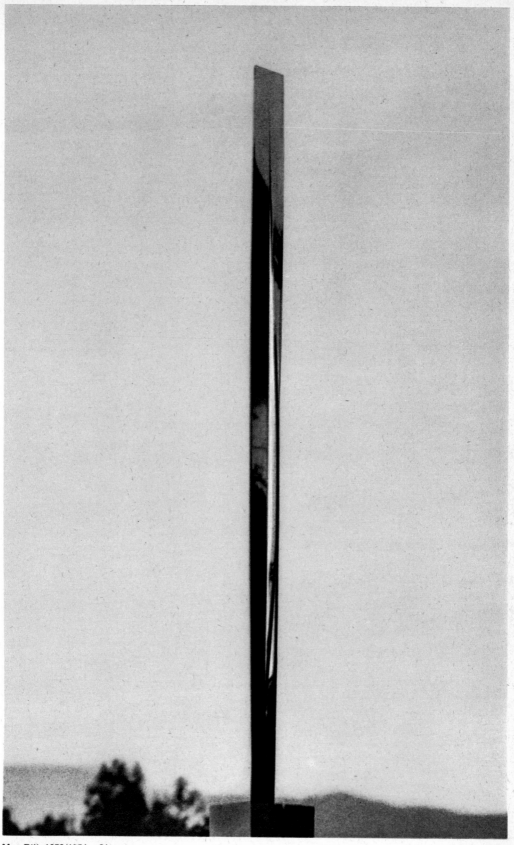

Max Bill, 1953/1954.   21

Bernhard Heiliger, 1955. 128

Henry Moore, 1950/1951.

Kenneth Armitage, 1957. 7

Pietro Consagra, 1957.   63

Karl Hartung, 1956.   1

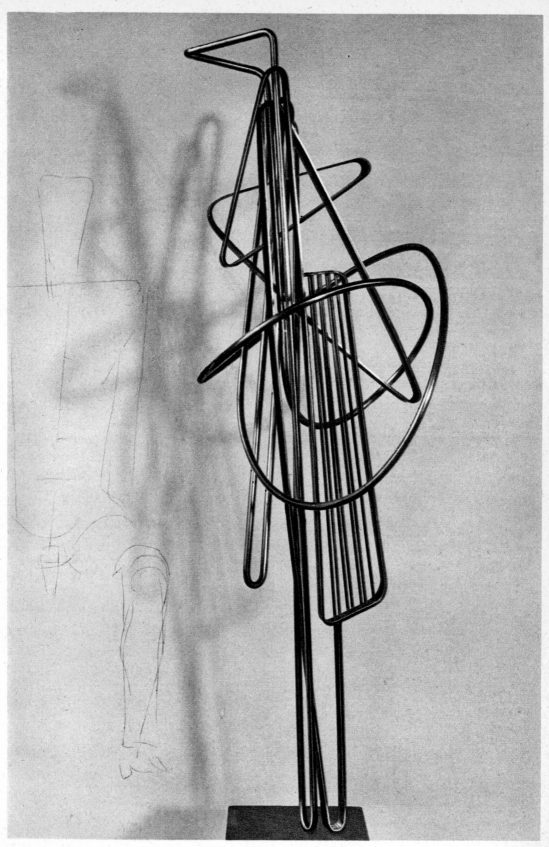

Hans Uhlmann, 1951. 315

Seymour Lipton, 1956. 181

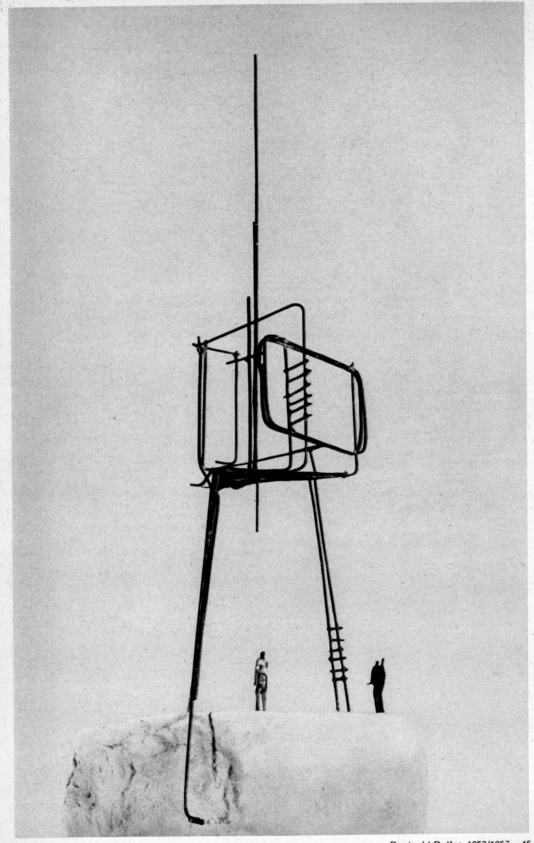

Reginald Butler, 1953/1957. 45

Acknowledgements for works loaned to the 1958 Brussels exhibition

Signora De Angeli, Milan; T. van Bakel, Waalre; Margarete Baumeister, Stuttgart; Henri Belien, Brussels; Baron Boël, Brussels; Carlo van den Bosch, Antwerp; M. Bourdon, Paris; J. Boussard, Paris; William A.M. Burden, New York; Cahen, Brussels; P. Campilli, Rome; A. Cavellini, Brescia; W. Copley, Songpont-sur-Orge; Marcel Cuvelier, Brussels; Bernheim Jeune Dauberville, Paris; Philippe Dotremont, Brussels; J. Dubourg, Paris; Trix Dürst-Hasse, Muttenz; P. Durand-Ruel, Paris; Dimitrios Evanguelidis, Athens; Marianne Feilchenfeldt, Zürich; B. J. Fisz, Paris; Shogetaro Fukushima, Izuyama; Van Geluwe, Brussels; Gedeon de Gerloczy, Budapest; Alvar Carillo Gil; Emilio Portes Gil, Mexico; V. W. van Gogh, Laren; R. Gonzalez, Arcueil; Fernand C. Graindorge, Liège; A. Gussoni, Milan; Wilhelm Hack, Cologne; M. R. Hauert, Paris; Rokubin Hayashi, Tokyo; A. Hecht, London; Tony Herbert, Courtrai; Cl. Hersent, Meudon; E. Hofer, Berlin; Edgar Horstmann, Hamburg; A. Hunter, London; Christian Isermeier, Hamburg; Pierre Janlet, Brussels; E. Jesi, Milan; Philip Johnson, New York; Jucker, Milan; Cléomire Jussiant, Antwerp; M. Kaganovitch, Paris; Matsutato Kawaguchi, Tokyo; Felix Klee, Berne; E. Kornfeld, Berne; Baroness Lambert, Brussels; H. Lütjens, Zürich; Max Lütze, Bad Homburg; A. Maeght, Paris; Oscar Mairlot, Verviers; Mme. Pierre Matisse, New York; G. Mattioli, Milan; Ragnar Moltzau, Oslo; Compagnie Nestlé – La Préalpina, Milan; Albert H. Newman, Chicago; Albert Niels; A. Orombelli, Milan; Annette Platou, Oslo; R. Penrose, London; N. Pisart-Fourez, Boulouris (Var); Regnault family, Laren; H. Robiliart, Brussels; Mme. Roëll-Jas, Scheveningen; Baroness A. de Rothschild, Reux (Calvados); P. Sacher-Stehlin, Basle; Tut Schlemmer, Stuttgart; Claude Spaak, Choisel; Otto Stangl, Munich; Karl Ströher, Darmstadt; G. Tosi, Milan; Burton Tremaine, Meriden; Prince I. Troubetzkoy, Paris; J. B. Urvater, Brussels; Vitali, Milan; S. C. Vitullo, Montrouge; Edith Vowinckel, Cologne; Gustav Zumsteg, Zürich.

Toulouse Lautrec Museum, Albi; Stedelijk Museum, Amsterdam; City of Antwerp; Kunstmuseum, Basel; Modern Art Gallery, Belgrade; Galerie des 20. Jahrhunderts, Berlin; Museum of Fine Arts, Berne; Kunsthalle, Bremen; Sammlung Ludwig Roselius, Roseliushaus, Bremen; Musées Royaux des Beaux-Arts de Belgique, Brussels; Allbright Art Gallery, Buffalo; Städtisches Museum, Duisburg; Stedelijk van Abbe Museum, Eindhoven; Folkwang-Museum, Essen; Musée des Beaux-Arts, Grenoble; Gemeente Museum, Den Haag; Frans Hals Museum, Haarlem; Städtisches Karl-Ernst-Osthaus-Museum, Hagen; Hamburger Kunsthalle, Hamburg; Niedersächsische Landesgalerie, Hanover; Wadsworth Atheneum Art Museum, Hartford; Museum of Modern Art, Cairo; Staatliche Kunsthalle, Karlsruhe; Wallraf-Richartz Museum, Cologne; Hermitage, Leningrad; Contemporary Art Society, London; Museo Nacional Arte Siglo XIX, Madrid; Civica Galleria d'Arte Moderna, Milan; Städtische Kunsthalle, Mannheim; Institute of Arts, Minneapolis; Walker Art Center, Minneapolis; Städtisches Museum, Munchen-Gladbach; Pushkin Museum, Moscow; State Tretiakov Gallery, Moscow; Martha Jackson Gallery, New York; Metropolitan Museum of Art, New York; Museum of Modern Art, New York; Sidney Janis Gallery, New York; Solomon R. Guggenheim Museum, New York; Nasjonalgalleriet, Oslo; National Gallery of Canada, Ottawa; Kröller-Müller Rijksmuseum, Otterlo; L'Association des Peintres Cartonniers, Paris; Musée National d'Art Moderne, Paris; Musée des Beaux-Arts de la Ville de Paris, Paris; Galerie Louis Carré, Paris; Galerie de France, Paris; Galerie Louise Leiris, Paris; Galerie Maeght, Paris; Galerie Pierre, Paris; Galerie Denise René, Paris; Musée Rodin, Paris; Galerie Dina Vierny, Paris; Philadelphia Museum of Art, Philadelphia; Narodni Galerie, Prague; Municipal Gallery of Modern Art, Rome; Boymans Museum, Rotterdam; Saarland-Museum, Saarbrücken; Gallery of Modern Art, Zagreb; Museo de Arte Moderne, Sao Paolo; Württembergische Staatsgalerie, Stuttgart; Kobutoya Gallery, Tokyo; Museum of Fine Arts, Turku; Munson-Williams-Proctor Institute, Utica; Commune de Watermael-Boitsfort; Österreichische Galerie, Vienna.

Biographies

prepared by R. Hammacher-Van den Brande

The number immediately following the date in the caption under each illustration provides a means of easy reference to the full description of each work which appears beneath the biography of its artist. These full descriptions are numbered consecutively throughout the biographies.

Henri-Georges Adam

Born in Paris, 1904, into a family of goldsmiths. Began with drawing and painting. His first exhibition was in 1935, and in the same year he won the Blumenthal Prize for print-making. Since 1940 he has been working at sculpture. He has done many designs for tapestries and has illustrated a number of books, including Gérard de Nerval's *Chimères*. Lives at Ville-du-Bois, Seine-et-Oise.
In the field of engraving Adam's specialities are etching and dry-point. The vigorous rhythm and strong black and white effects of his prints are found also on a much larger scale in his monumental tapestries.

1. Queen of Hearts 1949   *p. 205*
Aubusson tapestry, 110¹/₄″ × 137³/₄″. Signed and dated top right: "Adam 49"
In the artist's possession

Afro (Afro Basaldella)

Born in Udine, Italy, in 1912; brother of Mirko, the sculptor. Studied art in Venice. Decorated various public buildings in Udine. After his early Post-Impressionist works, he was attracted by Cubism, particularly that of Picasso and Braque. After the war, he worked his way progressively to a new aesthetic standpoint, achieving a personal style in which abstract form is combined with vigorous colouring. Stayed for a while in New York in 1950. In 1957 he designed the scenery for *Ritratto di Don Chisciotte* by Petrassi-Miloss. Now working in Rome.

2. Black news 1953   *p. 55*
Oil on canvas, 28³/₄″ × 40¹/₈″. Signed and dated at base on right: "Afro 1953"
Brescia, Cavellini collection

Mari Andriessen (Mari Silvester Andriessen)

Born at Haarlem, Holland, in 1897. Trained for a while in engineering, then studied sculpture in Amsterdam and Munich. His early work shows the influence of Romanesque and Gothic art. In sculpture, Andriessen is the representative of Dutch realism, which, under the influence of Professor Bronner of the Amsterdam Academy, strove to portray working-class life in sober, intimate Expressionism with little regard to problems of form but with monumental tendencies.
Andriessen's work reached its full maturity in the first years after the war in the execution of several monuments in homage to Dutch resistance. He lives in Haarlem.

3. Victim of shelling 1951   *p. 263*
Bronze, 70⁷/₈″
Antwerp, Museum of open-air sculpture, Middelheim

Karel Appel

Born at Amsterdam in 1921, and studied for a while at the Academy there. Was one of the founders of the international experimental group called *Cobra* (Copenhagen, Brussels, Amsterdam) and is a member of the Dutch group, *Reflex*. Won Unesco prize in 1954. Amongst his many mural works may be mentioned those at the National Museum in Amsterdam. Appel lives in Paris.
His works, the earlier of which resemble children's drawings, are characterised by large, brightly coloured surfaces which seem almost to be moulded out of the colour itself. The series of large portraits he executed in 1956 had lost nothing of his early vehemence.

4. Nude 1957   *p. 230*
Oil on canvas, 51¹/₈″ × 76³/₄″. Signed at base on left: "K. Appel 57"
Brussels, Willy Grubben collection

Alexandre Archipenko

Born in 1887 at Kiev, where he received his first lessons in art. He completed his studies in Moscow. In 1908 he settled in Paris, moving among the adherents of the budding Cubism and producing highly stylised human figures made up of concave and convex surfaces. About 1914, influenced by the Egyptian art he had discovered in the Louvre, he began his 'sculpto-painting', as he called it, an experiment in the combination of form and colour which exerted a considerable influence on the generations to come. In spite of his preoccupations as a theorist of Cubism, he gravitated from 1916 onwards towards a more traditional art. In Berlin from 1920 to 1923 he finally renounced Cubism in the search for more animated forms. Since 1923 he has been living in the United States, teaching, first at the Washington State University, then at the New Bauhaus, Chicago, and thirdly at his own school in New York. Lives at Woodstock, New York, where he runs a summer school.

5. *Female torso   1920/23*   *p. 247*
Bronze, Ht. 14". Signed on the base: "Archipenko"
Cologne, Wilhelm Hack collection

Mordechai Ardon

Born, 1896, at Tuchow in Poland. Studied first in Munich, then at the Bauhaus in Weimar where he met Klee, Kandinsky and Feininger. He then worked in Berlin and Jerusalem, where he occupied a post in the Ministry of Education and Culture. The influence of the Bauhaus is observable in the dramatic character of his Post-Expressionist art. For the last twenty years he has been working uninterruptedly in Israel.

6. *The Maggid's house   1954*   *p. 183*
Oil on canvas, 55¹/₈" × 42³/₄". Signed and dated at base on right: "Ardon 1954"
Brussels, Royal Belgian Museum of Fine Art

Kenneth Armitage

Born at Leeds in 1916. Studied at the Leeds College of Art, then went on to the Slade, where he stayed till 1939. He then served in the Army for seven years. In 1946 he began teaching sculpture at the Bath Academy of Art, Corsham, Wilts. In 1952 and 1954 he exhibited at the Venice Biennale. In 1953 he became Gregory Fellow at Leeds University. He works in London.
Armitage remains faithful to figurative art. His principal theme is the human figure. His groups are dominated by different planes, suggesting movement. The play of light on the rough but very subtle surfaces adds to the dynamic and expressive character of the work.

7. *Two figures walking   1957*   *p. 281*
Bronze, Ht. 47¹/₂", Wdth. 57¹/₈", Dpth. 20⁷/₈"
In the artist's possession

Hans Arp

Born in Strasbourg in 1887. Sculptor, painter, and poet. Studied in Strasbourg and Weimar. Went to Paris for the first time in 1907 and attended the Académie Julian. Got in touch with Apollinaire and his circle. Until 1922 he

lived chiefly in Switzerland and took part in the Dadaist manifestations in Zürich in 1916. In 1919 and 1920 he collaborated with Max Ernst in Cologne. In 1921 married the sculptor and poet Sophie Täuber. Settled in Paris in 1922 and joined the Surrealist movement. Since 1926 he has been living at Meudon except for the period of the war.
His apparent simplicity conceals a complex world of sexual symbolism and poetry.

8. *Configuration   1928*   *p. 141*
Painted wood, 57¹/₂" × 45¹/₄"
Basle, Art Museum (Emanuel Hoffman endowment)

9. *Metamorphosis   1935*   *p. 272*
Bronze, Ht. 27¹/₈", Wdth. 18¹/₈", Dpth. 16"
Liège, Fernand C. Graindorge collection

10. *Mirr   1936*   *p. 65*
Bronze, Ht. 13", Wdth. 14⁵/₈", Dpth. 18⁷/₈"
In the artist's possession

Francis Bacon

Born in Dublin, 1910. Self-taught, taking to painting about 1930. It was not till 1946 that he held his first exhibition.
He is one of the outstanding representatives of the romantic movement in England. Turning for preference to macabre hallucinations for its subjects, his art is haunted by anxiety and the dread of destruction. A world doomed to disintegration is symbolised by ghostlike persons, maimed and screaming, and by flayed animals. Bacon stands out from other English romantics by the vigour of his painting, the keen expressionism of the composition and his muted coloration.

11. *Study for figure   No. 6 1956*   *p. 239*
Oil on canvas 57⁵/₈" × 45¹/₄"
London, The Contemporary Art Society

Vojin Bakic

Born in Bjelovar in Croatia in 1915. Studied art in Zagreb. Travelled in Italy, France, and England. His sculpture is represented by several monuments in Yugoslavia.
After a Lyrico-Realist start, followed by a Neo-Cubist phase, he has reached, since 1950, what might be called his classic period, working in a synthetic style in pure and simple forms which maintain their contact with reality. His work belongs to the formal world of Brancusi and Arp.

12. *Reclining torso   1957*   *p. 273*
Stone, Ht. 13³/₄", Wdth. 46¹/₂"
In the artist's possession

Ernst Barlach

Born at Wedel in Holstein, 1870, Barlach went to the Kunstgewerbeschule, then the art-schools of Hamburg and Dresden. In 1895 he went to Paris and studied at the Académie Julian. Was in Berlin from 1898 to 1901. Travelled in Russia and Italy, and then in 1910 settled in Güstrow. In 1938 his works were designated 'degenerate art' and thrown out of public galleries. He died the same year in Rostock.

Sculptor, engraver, and poet, Barlach remained faithful all his life to monumental and concentrated forms. His essential style, severe and deliberately archaic, admitted no important modifications of his art, for its Expressionism was determined by his feelings concerning humanity and religion. Using bronze, and rehabilitating wood as a medium of sculpture, he undertook a wide range of sculptural subjects which he also drew. He remains one of the most outstanding artists of Germany between the two wars.

13. *The Avenger* 1923   *p. 245*
Bronze, Ht. 34¹/₄", Wdth. 15³/₄", Dpth. 20¹/₂"
Hamburg, Art Museum

Willi Baumeister

Born in 1889 in Stuttgart, where he studied as a pupil of Adolphe Hoelzel and became a friend of Schlemmer and Meyer-Amden. In 1912, on his first visit to Paris, he became acquainted with the work of Toulouse-Lautrec and Gauguin, and later, in 1914, that of Cézanne. In 1919 he produced the first of his wall-paintings, or *Mauerbilder*. During a visit to Paris in 1924, he made contact with Ozenfant, Le Corbusier and Léger. In 1928 he accepted a teaching post in Frankfurt, but was removed by the Nazis in 1933, his work being stigmatized as degenerate. During the period of artistic intolerance he worked quietly in obscurity in Stuttgart. He was given a professorship there in 1946. A book of his, *Das Unbekannte in der Kunst*, was published in 1947. He died in Stuttgart in 1955.
An artist of many gifts, he painted, illustrated books, and designed scenery, at the same time writing controversially on the politics of art. In his first *Mauerbilder* he tried to achieve a fusion of the wall and the picture upon it by exploiting the whole arsenal of Cubist forms. His later work oscillated between strict abstraction and figurative hints in a Surrealist atmosphere. Baumeister did much to establish the abstract art of his country.

14. *Composition: A design of walls (Mauerbild)* 1923   *p. 210*
Oil on wood, 46¹/₄" × 27"
Stuttgart, Mrs. Margarete Baumeister collection

15. *Nocturno* 1953   *p. 47*
51¹/₈" × 39³/₈". Signed and dated top right: "Baumeister 53"
Stuttgart, Mrs. Margarete Baumeister collection

Jean Bazaine

Born in Paris in 1904. First studied sculpture in the Ecole des Beaux-Arts, at the same time taking the degree of Licencié-ès-lettres; but since 1924 has given himself entirely to painting. In 1948 he published *Notes sur la peinture d'Aujourd'hui*. In 1950 he designed a series of stained glass windows for the church of Assy, and in 1951 a large ceramic mural and stained-glass windows for Audincourt.
His work, though originally very close to nature, cannot be called realistic. Since the war his style has moved towards pure and symbolic forms. Harmonious and richly coloured, his works reveal an extremely sensitive nature. He exerts a considerable influence on young painters in Paris.

16. *Earth and sky* 1950   *p. 214*
Oil on canvas, 76³/₄" × 51¹/₈". Signed at base on right:
"Bazaine"
Paris, Aimé Maeght collection

Max Beckmann

Born in Leipzig in 1884, Beckmann studied at the art-school in Weimar. His first stay in Paris was in 1903-1904. In 1906 he contributed to the exhibition of the *Berliner Sezession*. Was in Holland and Belgium as a soldier in 1914 and 1915. From 1915 to 1933 he lived in Frankfurt, where he taught painting in the art-school, but he was dismissed by the Nazis in 1933. He went to Berlin, then lived successively in Paris and Amsterdam, before finally settling in America in 1947, where he became professor in the Washington University, St. Louis. In 1949 he moved to New York, teaching at the Brooklyn Museum. In 1950 he was awarded the Carnegie Prize, and won another at the Venice Biennale. Died in New York, 1950.
Beckmann has never really been identified with any particular movement. Starting as a Post-Impressionist he then passed through an Expressionist period. Under the influence of the stark facts of war he moved towards a style of aggressive satire with affinities with Grosz and Dix. He contemplated fact and reported it objectively, impartially. In vast allegorical compositions and symbolic works like the *Perseus Triptych* he expresses his hatred at the same time as his love of mankind and life.

17. *Portrait of the artist with a saxophone* 1930   *p. 168*
Oil on canvas, 55¹/₈" × 27¹/₈"
Bremen, Art Museum

18. *Two women* 1940   *p. 30*
Oils, 31¹/₂" × 24³/₈"
Cologne, Wallraf-Richartz Museum

19. *Departure* 1932–35   *p. 167*
Oil on canvas – central panel, 84⁵/₈" × 45¹/₄".
Side panels, 84⁵/₈" × 39⁵/₈"
New York, Museum of Modern Art

Frits van den Berghe

Born in Ghent, 1883, son of a university librarian. Studied at the local art-school. In 1905 he settled in Laethem-Saint-Martin, and, with Permeke and the brothers Gustave and Léon de Smet, he formed the second Laethem group. In 1913 he spent six months in the United States, and during the first war he lived in Holland. Returning to Belgium in 1922 he lived at Ostend and at Laethem, and in 1925 he settled definitely in Ghent. A member of the *Groupe des IX, Art Vivant* and *Art Contemporain*. He died in 1939.
A particularly gifted artist, a man of great culture and remarkable intelligence, he was regarded as the spiritual head of the second Laethem group. His style at first closely resembled that of his colleagues but soon moved towards a fantastic Expressionism.

20. *Genealogy* 1929   *p. 173*
Oils, 57¹/₂" × 45". Signed at base on right: "F.V.Berghe"
Basle, Art Museum (Emmanuel Hoffmann endowment)

Max Bill

Born in 1908 at Winterthur in Switzerland, Bill was a product of the Zürich art-school and the Dessau Bauhaus. He has exerted a considerable influence in Zürich, where he has lived since 1929 and taught since 1944. In 1931 he became a member of the *Abstraction-Création* group in Paris. In 1951 he became head of the *Hochschule für Gestaltung* at Ulm, where he influenced many young artists, but he resigned in 1957 and is now working again in Zürich.

Architect, sculptor, painter, and writer, Bill is one of those men who can blend the mathematician's abstract thought with the creative activity of the artist. This aptitude is apparent in both his lectures and his writings and particularly in a treatise entitled *Die mathematische Denkweise in der Kunst unserer Zeit*, published in Zürich in 1949. His theories led him to pure abstract sculptures that might be called writings in space, in which form was dominated by line. Harmony and tension were combined in the grand manner in thoughtful compositions which demand the intellectual collaboration of the spectator.

21. Infinite surface, in the form of a column   1953/55   p. 277
Polished brass, 78³|₄″
In the artist's possession

Renato Birolli

Born in 1906 in Verona; studied there at the Academia Cignarelli. At eighteen he went to live in Milan. Joined the *Secondo Novecento* movement. In 1937 he founded the *Corrente* group and edited a review of that name. In 1947 he visited Paris for the first time, and came under the influence of Picasso and Matisse. Returning to Milan he became one of the moving spirits of the *Nuova Secessione*, whose works were shown in the 1948 Venice Biennale under the title *Fronte nuova delle Arti*. Progressively Birolli discarded all influences, finding his own form of abstraction, which is for him no more than a free rendering of reality.

22. Conflagration in the five lands   1957   p. 218
Oil on canvas, 47¹|₄″ × 55¹|₈″. Signed at base on right: "Birolli"
Rome, private collection

Hermann Blumenthal

Born at Essen in 1905. Began studying in Essen, then continued under Erwin Scharff in Berlin. Divided his life between Italy (Rome, Florence) and Berlin. Called up in 1940, he was killed on the Russian front in 1942.
This promising sculptor, who died all too young, was deeply involved in the problems of his day. His qualities were reflected in his calm figures, deliberately avoiding all pictorial effect.

23. Meditation   1928   p. 247
Bronze, Ht. 68¹|₂″
Hamburg, Hermann Blumenthal estate

Umberto Boccioni

Born at Reggio in Calabria in 1882; died at Sorte, Verona, in 1916. Technical studies at Catania and at Rome in 1898 where he made friends with Severini and Balla, who had returned from Paris, and who taught him the laws of Pointillism, then fashionable in France. After a visit to Paris and a short stay in Russia, he settled in Milan in 1908. There he met Marinetti, who in 1909 launched the first Futurist manifesto. In 1910, with Carrà, Russolo, Severini, and Balla, he signed the *Manifesto of Futurist Painters*. Boccioni became the chief theorist of the movement. In 1912 he published his *Technical Manifesto of Futurist Sculptors*, and in 1914 his *Futurist Painting and Sculpture*.

24. Street machine   1911   p. 136
Oil on canvas, 39³|₈″ × 31¹|₂″
Basle, private collection

25. A cyclist – a study in dynamism   1913   p. 137
Oil on canvas, 27⁵|₈″ × 37³|₈″
Milan, Gianni Mattioli collection

26. Study in dynamism – a human body   1913   p. 249
Bronze, Ht. 44¹|₂″, Wdth. 35³|₈″, Dpth. 16¹|₈″
Milan, Civic Gallery of Modern Art

Herbert Boeckl

Born at Klagenfurt in Austria in 1894. He began to study architecture, but gave it up to devote himself entirely to painting.
His style, influenced at first by Cézanne, developed rapidly towards a sober Expressionism. He travelled in Sicily and Germany and worked for a while in Paris. Returning to Austria he produced Expressionistic works which blended the main European currents in painting with the tendencies prevailing in modern Austria.
After a journey to Spain in 1952 he executed some mural paintings for the Benedictine chapel at Seckau. These frescoes form one of the most important examples of modern religious art in Austria. He was several times Rector of the Academy of Fine Arts, Vienna, where he was made professor in 1935.

27. The temptation of Saint Anthony   1957   p. 234
Oil on canvas, 71⁵|₈″ × 59⁷|₈″
In the artist's possession

Pierre Bonnard

Born at Fontenay-aux-Roses, not far from Paris, in 1867; died at Le Cannet in 1947. While a law student in Paris, he attended the Académie Julian as an amateur. Finally he abandoned the law and joined a group called the *Nabis* (prophets). Had much in common with Maurice Denis, Sérusier, Vuillard, and Toulouse-Lautrec. During this period Bonnard was particularly interested in popular art, doing sketches for posters, designs for furniture, book illustrations, etc, and working for a marionette theatre. In the wake of Post-Impressionism, he became from 1899 onwards the painter of interiors *par excellence*.
His relations with Renoir between 1890 and 1892 have left their mark, but both in palette and composition he belongs to the 20th century. Bonnard stands half-way between Impressionism and Fauvism.

28. Street scene   1907   p. 92
Oil on canvas, 39³|₈″ × 31⁷|₈″. Signed at base on left: Bonnard Zürich, of Mrs. M. Feilchenfeldt collection

29. Nude bathing   Before 1937   p. 93
Oil on canvas, 36⁵|₈″ × 57⁷|₈″. Signed at base on right: "Bonnard"

30. Flowery meadow   p. 94
Oil on canvas, 36⁵|₈″ × 36¹|₄″
Bonnard estate

31. Dining room   p. 94
Oil on canvas, 33¹|₈″ × 39³|₈″. Signed at base on left: "Bonnard"
Bonnard estate

Carlos Botelho

Born in Lisbon in 1899, he was brought up in an intellectual and musical atmosphere, and music had a considerable influence on his artistic development. Studied in Lisbon and then in Paris, where he worked some time, amongst other things on the Portuguese pavilion in the Exposition Coloniale of 1921 and on the Exposition Universelle of 1937. Was for a while in Holland and Belgium before returning to Portugal. Won the Sousa Cardosa prize in 1939 and the Colombano prize in 1940. Lives in Lisbon. Botelho was influenced by Picasso and Braque on the one hand and Van Gogh on the other. Characterised at first by a lyrical Post-Impressionism, his style has recently moved towards a more delicate palette and a more strictly synthetic form in which the figurative theme has practically disappeared.

32. Old Street 1955
Gouache, 28³|₄″ × 20⁷|₈″. Signed at base on right: "Botelho"
In the artist's possession

p. 215

Constantin Brancusi

Born at Pestisani Gorj in Rumania in 1876. His technical proficiency soon attracted attention when he studied at Bucharest and at Cracow. In 1902 he undertook the long journey to Paris on foot, arriving in 1904 after having passed through Munich, Zürich, and Basle. There he lived an almost legendary life till his death in 1957. In 1906 he met Rodin, but declined to collaborate with him. He encouraged his friend Modigliani to turn to sculpture. Brancusi's work was never abstract. It was inspired by an inward need to create forms which are pure, absolute, and powerful. The form, being restrained beneath its often polished surface, is very intense. A secluded figure while still alive, Brancusi has exerted a considerable influence on modern art, both abstract and figurative.

33. Torso of a young man 1924
Polished bronze, Ht. 19⁵|₈″
New York, Mr. & Mrs. George W. Staempfli collection

p. 269

34. Seal 1943
Grey marble, Ht. 63″, Wdth. 43¹|₄″, Dpth. 13³|₈″
Paris, National Museum of Modern Art

p. 64

35. Bird in space 1925
Copper, Ht. 71⁵|₈″
New York, Mr. & Mrs. William A.M.Burden collection

p. 269

Georges Braque

Born in Argenteuil in 1882, the son of a house-painter. Was educated in Le Havre and went to Paris in 1900 to continue his studies. After a 'fauve' period, he joined with Picasso, in 1907, in promoting a new style which the critics christened 'Cubism'. In 1912 he was one of the first to undertake 'collages'. After being seriously wounded in the first world war he resumed work straightaway and designed sets for Diaghilev's ballets. Braque's art, often inspired by ancient Greece, finds expression in both painting and sculpture; his engravings are also very important. Of recent years, still in full command of his technique, he has been working on etchings, lithographs, stage décors and the decoration of a large ceiling in the Louvre. In 1948 he was awarded the Grand Prix of the Venice Biennale. Lives in Paris.

36. Antwerp harbour 1906
Oil on canvas, 51⁵|₈″ × 24″
Ottawa National Gallery of Canada

p. 100

37. Landscape – Laroche-Guyon 1909
Oil on canvas, 25⁵|₈″ × 21¹|₄″
New York, Mr. & Mrs. George W. Staempfli collection

p. 111

38. Girl with guitar 1913
Oil on canvas, 51¹|₈″ × 29¹|₈″. Signed on the back: "Braque"
Paris, National Museum of Modern Art

p. 13

39. Still life on marble table 1925
Oil on canvas, 51¹|₈″ × 29¹|₈″. Signed and dated at base on right: "G. Braque 1925"
Paris, National Museum of Modern Art

p. 121

40. Horse's head 1943
Bronze, Ht. 17³|₈″, Wdth. 35³|₈″. Signed centre bottom: "G. Braque"
Paris, Aimé Maeght collection

p. 253

41. Bird and its nest 1956
Oil on canvas, 51¹|₈″ × 68¹|₄″. Signed at base on left: "G. Braque"
In the artist's possession

p. 240

42. The red table-cloth 1956
Oil on canvas, 51¹|₈″ × 63³|₄″. Signed at base on left: "G. Braque"
Paris, Aimé Maeght collection

p. 120

Isaac Israïlevitch Brodsky

Born in Leningrad in 1884. After studying at the art school and academy in Odessa, Brodsky took part in several exhibitions in the Soviet Union and abroad (Eastern Germany, Finland, Hungary, India). His work was shown at the XIXth Venice Biennale and the Paris Exposition of 1937. He died in Leningrad in 1939.

43. Lenin at the Smolny Institute 1930
Signed and dated at base on left: "Brodsky 30"
Moscow, Tretiakov Museum

p. 201

Jean Brusselmans

Born in Brussels in 1884. Worked at engraving and lithography, at the same time studying painting in evening classes at the Academy in Brussels. Before long he was devoting himself entirely to painting. Died in 1953 at Dilbeek near Brussels where he had worked for the greater part of his life.

After his Post-Impressionist beginnings he soon moved towards an Expressionism that was apparently cold and severe. His last works, in which the object takes on a primordial importance, belong to what might be called 'expressive realism'. Brusselmans, whose favourite subjects were the Brabant landscape and the North Sea, is a solitary figure in Flemish Expressionism.

44. Winter landscape 1939
Oil on canvas, 40¹|₈″ × 43¹|₄″. Signed and dated at base on right: "Jean Brusselmans 1939"
Courtrai, Tony Herbert collection

p. 172

Reginald Butler

Born at Buntingford, Herts. in 1913. Started working as architect and engineer in 1937. In 1950 he gave up architecture to devote himself entirely to sculpture. He was Gregory Fellow at Leeds University from 1950 to 1953. In 1953 he won an international prize for his monument to the Unknown Political Prisoner. Lives at Berkhamsted.

Butler's approach is from architecture and engineering. His figures are the expression of a rivalry between transparent forms in steel and solid modelling in bronze. Having gone through a Constructivist period (to which his Unknown Political Prisoner belongs) he passed on to figurative work.

45. The unknown political prisoner 1957   *p. 288*
Version of original project of 1953. Plaster, steel and bronze, Ht. 84″, Wdth. 29⁷/₈″
In the artist's possession

Alexander Calder

Born in Philadelphia in 1898 into a family of sculptors. Studied engineering before going on to painting and later metal-work. From 1926 he lived for twelve years in Paris, where he got to know the Surrealists and the Dadaists (Arp and Miro) and the principal representatives of the *De Stijl* movement (Mondrian and Van Doesburg). In 1928 he exhibited for the first time in New York, showing his wire sculptures. Increasingly drawn to non-figurative art, he constructed his first mobiles in 1932. His playful abstractions in space often recall the natural elements – the wind, water, leaves – although there is no question of imitation.

46. Empennage 1954   *p. 69*
Mobile on base, 118¹/₈″ × 185″
Paris, Galerie Maeght

47. The apostrophe 1958   *p. 274*
Mobile, Ht. 47¹/₄″, Wdth. 236¹/₄″
In the artist's possession

Massimo Campigli

Born in Florence in 1895. Self-taught. Worked as a journalist in Milan from 1915 to 1917. In 1919 he went to Paris and took up painting, coming under the influence of Picasso's neo-classical work. First exhibition in Paris in 1923. Travelled considerably in Europe and the United States. From 1939 to 1948 he was working in Milan. Then he returned to Paris, where he is now living.
Mixing in Carrà's circle, he has nonetheless acquired an archaistic style of his own, influenced by Etruscan and Cretan culture and the Ecole de Paris.

48. Female acrobats 1926   *p. 145*
Oil on canvas, 51¹/₈″ × 34⁵/₈″. Signed and dated at base on left: "M. Campigli 1926"
Milan, Dr. Emilio Jesi collection

Giuseppe Capogrossi

Born in Rome in 1900. Took a degree in law, but then devoted himself to painting. Lived in Paris from 1927 to 1932. With the painters Cagli and Cavalli he founded the *Gruppo Romano*. Undergoing a slow evolution, he turned in 1949 to abstract work. Has exhibited in the Venice Biennale. Lives in Rome.
Inspired by ancient prints and botanical motives, Capogrossi creates infinite variations on a constantly repeated trident element, which gives the work a somewhat decorative character.

49. Surfaces 195 1956   *p. 219*
Oil on canvas, 57⁷/₈″ × 38¹/₈″
Milan, Galleria de Navigio

Carlo Carrà

Born at Quargnento, near Alessandria, in 1881; he began painting very young. Studied at the Accademia Brera, Milan. First visited Paris and London in 1900. Under the influence of Seurat was first interested in Divisionist experiments before attaching himself to Futurism. In 1910 he signed the *Manifesto of the Futurist Painters*, and from this time onward his painting and writing were entirely dedicated to that movement. From 1911 to 1914 he was in Paris, associating with Apollinaire, Picasso, and the Cubists. In 1917, having met Chirico at Ferrara, he transferred to the *Pittura Metafisica*, and from 1919, when he became associated with the *Valori Plastici* group, he adopted a style of archaistic realism.
Teaching in Milan, Carrà exerted a decisive influence on the younger painters there between the two wars. He has written a study of Giotto and many articles.

50. Funeral of the anarchist, Galli 1911   *p. 37*
Oil on canvas 78″ × 102″. Signed at base on left: "Carra"
New York, Museum of Modern Art (Lillie P. Bliss Bequest)

51. The metaphysical muse 1917   *p. 143*
Oil on canvas. 35″ × 25⁵/₈″. Signed and dated at base on right: Carra 1917
Milan, Dr. Emilio Jesi collection

Paul Cézanne

Born in 1839 in Aix-en-Provence, the son of a hatter turned banker, Cézanne attended Gibert's classes at the drawing school of Aix and followed David's academic principles. After winning second prize for drawing, he matriculated and became a law student. In 1861 his father let him go to Paris, where he joined the Atelier Suisse and met Guillaumin who introduced him to Pissarro. He lived modestly, often visited the Louvre and failed to get into the Ecole des Beaux-Arts. Discouraged, he became a clerk in his father's bank at Aix, though continuing to draw and paint. In 1862 he returned to Paris. In 1866 he met Manet who admired his still-life paintings. In 1870, fleeing from the war, he went to the Midi where he began to paint in the open air. Then for two years he lived at Auvers, near Guillaumin and Pissarro, painting among other things *La Maison du Pendu*, which marked the transition between his later style and Impressionism. From 1879 his art developed and expanded. In 1882 he moved to Provence where he lived for some years in complete isolation. This was a period of great creative activity; his own classical style evolved although he was still obsessed by doubt. In 1895 A. Vollard organized an exhibition of Cézanne's work which did little to advance his reputation except among artists. In 1899 he moved to Aix where he lived until his death in almost total solitude, although his fame spread throughout the world. At the time of his death his influence was already considerable.
Although his work foreshadowed pure painting and abstraction, he strove to make faithful copies of reality and translate light into paint. In wanting to achieve truth, he surpassed the realistic impressionism of his day. In his own words, he was 'the primitive of a new art'. In the 20th century more than one movement has been based on Cézanne; Fauvists, Cubists, abstract and neo-classical painters all owe a debt to him. With him a whole epoch of art was closed and a new one opened.

52. Mardi Gras 1888   *p. 89*
Oil on canvas, 48³/₈″ × 31⁷/₈″
Moscow, Pushkin Museum

53. Le Mont Sainte-Victoire   1904   p. 90
Oil on canvas, 27⁵/₈″ × 35³/₈″
*Philadelphia, Philadelphia Museum of Art. Commissioners of
Fairmount Park, Georges W. Elkins collection, courtesy of the
Philadelphia Museum of Art*

54. Le Clos des Mathurins   c. 1875   p. 91
Oil on canvas, 20⁷/₈″ × 28″
Moscow, Pushkin Museum

Ivan Dmitrievitch Chadr (Ivanov)

Born in Tatachinsku, Sciadrinsk, in Russia in 1887. Died
in Moscow, 1941. Studied at the art-school in Ekaterin-
burg. Worked in Paris from 1910 to 1912. Contributed
to many important exhibitions in Russia and elsewhere,
notably to the 14th, 16th, and 18th Venice Biennales, and
exhibited in the Exposition Universelle, Paris, 1937.

55. Gorky   1939   p. 266
Bronze, Ht. 27⁵/₈″, Wdth. 11³/₄″, Dpth. 13³/₄″
Moscow, Tretiakov Museum

Lynn Chadwick

Born in London in 1914. Studied architecture, and only
took up sculpture in 1945. His first mobiles to some extent
betrayed the influence of Calder and Gonzalez.
In recent years Chadwick has produced a series of bold
figures, constructed in a steel framework of geometrical
delineation, and he also uses copper, bronze, wrought
iron, and plaster, sometimes with the addition of bits of
glass. In 1956 he won the Grand Prix for sculpture at the
Venice Biennale. He lives in Gloucestershire.

56. Alabama moon   1957   p. 287
Iron, Ht. 57⁷/₈″
In the artist's possession

Marc Chagall

Born in 1887 in the ghetto of Vitebsk. Studied in St. Petersburg. When he arrived in Paris in about 1910, Cubism
was in full swing. Without coming under the influence of
either Picasso or Braque, he nevertheless intuitively
adopted their conception of space. Returning to Russia in
1914 he was offered, like Kandinsky, Pevsner, and Gabo,
a teaching post in his native country. At the same time he
worked for the Jewish theatre in Moscow. In the uphea-
vals of cultural policy in 1923 he was forced to leave the
country. Passing through Berlin he returned to Paris. In
1941 he took refuge in America but returned to France
in 1947, settling in Vence, where he is still working.
Chagall derives his inspiration chiefly from the symbolism
of icons, Jewish mysticism and memories of youth. His
paintings are imbued with personal lyricism and warm,
rich colouration. He introduces symbols that have sprung
from his fertile imagination. Such is the poetry of his art
that it expresses with an almost metaphysical fervour his
love of nature and the mysteries of life.

57. I and the village   1911   p. 18
Oil on canvas, 75⁵/₈″ × 59¹/₈″. Signed and dated at base on
right: "Chagall 1911 Paris"
*New York, Museum of Modern Art (Mrs. Simon Guggen-
heim Fund)*

58. Pregnant woman (Maternity)   1913   p. 182
Oil on canvas, 76³/₈″ × 45¹/₄″. Signed and dated, centre base:
"Chagall 1913"
*Property of the Dutch state (on loan to the Stedelijk Museum,
Amsterdam)*

59. The Big Top   1956   p. 183
Oil on canvas, 59″ × 122″. Signed and dated at base on right:
"Marc Chagall 1956"
Paris, Maeght Gallery

Giorgio de Chirico

Born at Volo on the Thessalonian coast of Greece in 1888.
His father, a Sicilian, was a railway engineer. Studied at
Athens and Munich. During his first stay in Paris, from
1911 to 1915, he met Apollinaire, Picasso, Max Jacob and
Maurice Raynal. Returning to Italy, he stayed there until
1924. Founder of the *Pittura Metafisica*. He met Carrà in
Ferrara and in 1919 joined the *Valori Plastici* group. In 1924
he went to live in Paris for the second time. In 1939 he
settled in Rome, where he is now working.
The *Pittura Metafisica* was a revolt against the dynamism
of Futurism. In his compositions, with their architectural
and monumental elements, dummies, and other anoma-
lous subjects altogether out of keeping with reality, he
creates a 'counter-reality' which is the forerunner of
Surrealism. Between 1920 and 1925 his conceptions underwent a change which led him towards a Classico-Baroque
style. Repudiating his past, he now produced work devoid
of the magic and fantastic atmosphere of his metaphysical
period. It is the work of the earlier years, i. e. before
1925, which made such a contribution to Italy's part in
the resurgence of modern art.

60. Place d'Italie   1912   p. 143
Oil on canvas, 18¹/₂″ × 22¹/₂″. Signed and dated at base on
right: Chirico 1912
Milan, Dr. Emilio Jesi collection

61. Poet and philosopher   1914   p. 142
Oil on canvas, 31⁷/₈″ × 25⁵/₈″
Milan, Alfonso Orombelli collection

62. Evangelical still life   1917   p. 38
Oil on canvas, 35³/₈″ × 23⁵/₈″
Milan, private collection

Pietro Consagra

Born at Mazara del Vallo in Sicily in 1920, he studied at
Palermo. Went to Rome in 1944, making friends with
Guttuso and other artists of the avant-garde. In 1947 he
founded the *Forma* group, the first outpost of non-figurative art in Italy.
Leaning first towards Cubism, he rapidly moved on to
abstract art. His two-dimensional sculpture retains a contact with reality, seeking inspiration from the relations
between man and the community. Consagra has published
many articles and essays in which he explains his attitude
to modern sculpture.

63. Conversation before the mirror   1957   p. 282
Bronze, Ht. 56¹/₄″, Wdth. 41″
In the artist's possession

Lovis Corinth

Born in 1858 at Tapiau in East Prussia. Studied at Königsberg, Munich, Antwerp, and Paris. About 1900 he settled in Berlin. His first period was characterised by a Naturalist-Impressionist style and he is sometimes associated with Max Liebermann as representative of German Impressionism. After a stroke in 1911 the style of his painting changed entirely. From 1919 he was often at Walchensee in Bavaria, where he painted many landscapes. Exhausted by illness and work, he died in 1925 at Zandvoort in Holland.

Outstripping that of his contemporaries who remained attached to the 19th century, his art belongs to our time rather than theirs. The vitality of his painting, particularly in his last Walchensee landscapes, is not derived from the subject but from the power of his expression and the richness of his colouring.

64. Walchensee and golden meadow 1921   p. 99
Oil on canvas, 27⁵/₈″ × 33¹/₂″. Signed and dated at base on left:
"Lovis Corinth 1921"
Munich, Bavarian State Art collection

Corneille (Cornelis van Beverloo)

Born at Liège of Dutch parents in 1922. Studied drawing in Amsterdam. As a painter he is self-taught. In Holland he founded, with Appel and Constant, the experimental *Reflex* group. In 1948 he was one of the founders of the international group *Cobra*. Now living in Paris.

Less aggressive and more poetic than his colleagues in these experimental groups, his early work has certain affinities with Miró and Klee, but his later works show a departure from this style.

65. Hostile city 1954   p. 231
Oil on canvas, 35⁷/₈″ × 50¹/₂″. Signed and dated, top left:
"Corneille 54"
Eindhoven, Stedelijk van Abbe Museum

Theodor Csontvary
(Michael Theodore Kosztka)

Born at Kisszeben in northern Hungary in 1853; was a civil servant, a law student, and a chemist before taking up painting. According to his own account he was over forty when a 'mysterious voice' urged him to turn to art. He then went to study at Munich, Karlsruhe, Düsseldorf and the Académie Julian in Paris. Travelled in Italy, Greece, Egypt and the East, seeking inspiration in nature. The lyrical *Promenade près de la mer* is his last picture, for he produced nothing in the remaining ten years of his life. He died at Budapest in 1919.

Csontvary is a strange and exceptional figure in Hungarian painting. A mystic, pantheistic visionary, he attempted in his large canvasses to be realistic while creating a fantastic world, often painted in a naïve style. He gave free rein to his fertile imagination and cosmic ideas in visionary works with supernatural overtones which sometimes came near to Surrealism. His works have the poetic atmosphere and narrative character of Persian tales.

66. Outing on horseback 1907   p. 97
Oil on canvas, 33¹/₂″ × 55¹/₈″
Budapest, Gedeon de Gerloczy collection

Salvador Dali

Born in 1904 at Figueiras near Barcelona. Studied at Madrid. In 1920 became interested in Futurism, which led him to Cubism, and in the metaphysical work of De Chirico and Carrà. After painting in various styles, Realism, Cubism, and Neo-Classicism, he found his personal style when, in 1928, he made contact with Picasso and the Surrealists. In 1929 he made a film with Luis Bunuel, *Le Chien Andalou*, and another in 1931, *L'Age d'Or*. In 1934 he visited the United States, and in 1937 Italy, where he was profoundly impressed by the Renaissance. He paints murals (London 1936, New York 1942), designs costumes and décors for ballets *(Labyrinthe, Colloquia Sentimenta, Tristan Le Fou, Les Vendages)*, illustrates books *(Les Chants du Maldoror, the Divine Comedy, Don Quixote)*, designs jewellery and writes sensational books. Despite his taste for scandal and publicity, no one can deny the eminent place he occupies in the Surrealist movement.

Drawing and painting with extraordinary virtuosity he composes fantastic works in a realistic style which often contains a deeply poetic element. Of recent years he has been inclined to use, in his large works, religious themes taken from the New Testament.

67. Premonition of civil war 1936   p. 44
Oil on canvas, 43¹/₄″ × 33¹/₈″
Philadelphia, Philadelphia Museum of Art (Louise and Walter Arensberg collection)

68. The temptation of St Anthony 1946   p. 188
Oil on canvas, 35³/₈″ × 47¹/₄″. Signed and dated at base on right: "Salvador Dali 46"
Brussels, H. Robiliart collection

Alexandre Alexeivitch Deineka

Born at Kursk in 1899. Studied at the Kharkov and Vkhutemas art schools. He has contributed to important exhibitions in Russia and elsewhere, particularly in East Germany, Hungary, Austria, Czechoslovakia, and Yugoslavia, and also to several Venice Biennales and to the Paris Exposition Universelle in 1937. Lives in Moscow.

69. The Defence of Petrograd 1928   p. 204
Oil on canvas, 85³/₈″ × 139³/₈″. Signed and dated at base on right: "Deineka 1928"
Moscow, Tretiakov Museum

Robert Delaunay

Born in Paris in 1885, Delaunay received his first artistic education in an *atelier de décoration*. During a stay in Brittany he came in contact with the Pont-Aven group and with Gauguin. After a Neo-impressionist start, he became one of the pioneers of Cubism, and in 1911 got into contact with Kandinsky. Between 1911 and 1913 he painted his first abstract pictures. He was invited in 1911 to contribute to the *Blaue Reiter* exhibition in Munich. In 1913 he went to Berlin with Apollinaire and exhibited in the *Sturm* gallery. This was the beginning of the *formes circulaires* period. Was in Spain during the 1914–1918 war, returning to Paris in 1921. In 1937 he undertook several huge decorative works for the Exposition Universelle in Paris. Died at Montpellier in 1941.

Influenced by Seurat's work and by Chevreul's aesthetic ideas, he was interested in the theories relating to the composition of colours. He broke colours up, without going as far as Pointillism. In his *Windows* he experiments with the simultaneous contrast of colours. His first truly abstract works exerted a considerable influence, particularly in Germany (Kandinsky, Klee).

Delaunay was the chief representative of the movement which Apollinaire called 'Orphisme', and which assigned the first importance to colour. Colour became 'the shape and the object'. His essays, so far unpublished, describe his theories and the results of his experiments. He contributed largely to the establishment of abstract art.

70. *The Eiffel Tower 1910* p. 131
Oil on canvas, 78″ × 53¹⁄₂″. Signed and dated at base on right: "R. Delaunay 1910", at base on left: "La Tour 1910"
New York, The Solomon R. Guggenheim Museum

71. *A window 1912/1913* p. 132
Oil on canvas. On the back: "Une fenêtre, étude pour les trois fenêtres". Signed: "Delaunay" and "1912, Paris 1913"
Paris, National Museum of Modern Art

Paul Delvaux

Born at Antheit, near Huy in Belgium, in 1897, the son of a lawyer. Studied at the Académie des Beaux-Arts in Brussels. At first he painted portraits, landscapes, and sea-scapes in the style of Permeke. Travelling in France and Italy he discovered Surrealism, and in particular the work of Chirico. In 1930 he turned towards Surrealism and took part in a number of undertakings on behalf of the movement, though he never adhered strictly to its programme. Executed important murals at the Ostend Kuursaal and in a private house in Brussels. Paul Delvaux lives in Brussels, where he teaches at the Institut National Supérieur d'Architecture et des Arts Décoratifs.

Delvaux's Surrealism draws its inspiration from the subconscious. He likes to place dreaming, often naked figures, meticulously painted, in incongruous surroundings, such as a railway station or a classical building. The atmosphere is strange and poetic. He is one of the outstanding figures of Belgian Surrealism.

72. *Hands 1941* p. 190
Oil on canvas, 43¹⁄₄″ × 51¹⁄₈″. Signed and dated, centre base: "P. Delvaux 5. 6. 41"
Choisel, Claude Spaak collection

André Derain

Born in 1880 at Chatou, near Versailles. Encouraged by Vlaminck, he started painting, and also worked at sculpture, print-making, décor and book-illustration. In 1904 he joined the *Fauves*, getting to know Matisse, Picasso and Braque. He stayed in the movement till 1905, painting with vigorous colours. From 1908, under the influence of Cézanne and Negro sculpture, his compositions became geometric in concept, more disciplined in colour, almost approaching Cubism. After the first war he turned to classical art and produced a series of powerful works in an archaistic idiom, nudes, portraits, landscapes, and still-lives. He died in 1954.

An eclectic artist, Derain was too prone to submit to the intellectual fashions of the age, and sought out old techniques in order to adapt them to the needs of contemporary life. His lack of self-confidence caused him to waste his own real gifts and prevented him from becoming a major artist of his period.

73. *Westminster Bridge 1907* p. 101
Oil on canvas, 31⁷⁄₈″ × 39³⁄₈″. Signed at base on right: "Derain"
Paris, private collection

74. *The billiard-saloon 1913* p. 122
Oil on canvas, 55¹⁄₈″ × 34⁵⁄₈″
Tokyo, Kabutoya Gallery

Cevat Dereli

Born at Rize in Turkey in 1900. Studied art. Lived in Paris from 1924 to 1928. One of the founders in 1928 of a group of independent painters and sculptors. Contributed to numerous exhibitions, including the 1956 Venice Biennale. Since 1928 he has taught painting in the art-school at Istanbul.

Influenced at first by European primitives and Turkish miniature painters, he eventually developed a sober Expressionism.

75. *Landscape 1956* p. 172
Oil on canvas, 33¹⁄₂″ × 48″. Signed and dated at base on right: "C. Dereli 1956"
Istanbul, Museum of Painting and Sculpture

Charles Despiau

Born in 1874 at Mont-de-Morsan, where his father and grandfather were stucco-workers. Went to Paris in 1891 and attended the Ecole des Arts Décoratifs and the Ecole des Beaux-Arts. He won no prizes and earned his living by colouring post-cards. In 1903 his bust of Mme. Despiau was exhibited at the Belgian National Gallery, but it was not until the following year that he made his mark with *La Petite Fille des Landes*. Rodin admired him and they collaborated for some time. By the first war Despiau was fully master of his art. Besides many sensitive intimate portraits, which gave new life to the tradition of portraiture in stone, he also did some large sculptures and left some fine drawings.

76. *Mme. Agnes Meyer 1929* p. 242
Bronze, Ht. 24³⁄₈″, Wdth. 7¹⁄₂″
Paris, National Museum of Modern Art

Otto Dix

Born in 1891 at Unterhausen in Thuringia. Studied in Dresden and Düsseldorf. Settled in Berlin, then in 1927 moved to Dresden, where he became professor at the Academy. Forced to resign in 1933. Served in the German army during the last war and then, in 1946, went to Hemmenhofen where he is still living.

Dix began working in a realistic style, as in his portrait of his parents. His keen sense of reality and truth led him to a technique known as *Neue Sachlichkeit*. As with Grosz, his work provides a satirical commentary on wartime and post-war life.

77. Portrait of my parents 1924   *p. 196*
Oil on canvas, 46^1/$_2$"×51". Inscription and date top right
Hanover, State Gallery of Lower Saxony

Kees van Dongen

Born in 1877 at Delshaven near Rotterdam. Extremely gifted, he started drawing and painting in his childhood. Going to live in Paris, he led the miserable life of the penniless artist in Montmartre, sometimes earning his living as a house-painter, sometimes as a porter at Les Halles. He liked to sketch on café terraces, and, like Steinlen and Jacques Villon, contributed to satirical newspapers. From 1905 he was an enthusiastic supporter of Fauvism and contributed to the exhibitions of the movement. After the first war, he became chiefly famous for his portraits, often cruel, of famous people. Lives in Paris.

78. Anita 1905/1906   *p. 99*
Oil on canvas, 31^7/$_8$"×51^1/$_8$". Signed on centre base: "van Dongen"
In the artist's possession

Jean Dubuffet

Born at Le Havre in 1901. Went to Paris in 1918 and began studying art. From 1924 he divided his time between painting and commerce. In 1934 he produced some masks, marionettes and mouldings. His real artistic career only began in 1942 when he started to concentrate on painting and lithography. But he still painted only for himself, thinking himself too old for a new career. His first exhibition at the Drouin Gallery in 1944 was immensely successful. But from 1946 Dubuffet became a constant target for the newspaper critics, after his exhibition *Mirobolus, Macadam et Cie.* Between 1947 and 1949 he undertook several journeys in the Sahara, returning with an important series of drawings and *gouaches.* In 1955 he settled at Vence, and it was from there that he issued his *assemblages d'empreintes.* His work is influenced by *l'art brut* (the work of recluses, eccentrics, and mental cases) of which he possesses a vast collection. He likes experimenting with unusual materials such as sand, tar, charcoal, varnish, glass and all sorts of objects which he applies with a trowel or by hand, adding colour sparingly. The total effect makes up a magical, primitive world. He draws his inspiration as much from the phenomena of the visible world and the irrational and instinctive elements within himself as from the properties of his materials. His ambiguous work is based not on reason but on sensibility and intuition. He is one of the most important and complex artists of today.

79. Woman chanting (Reddish nude) 1945   *p. 233*
Oil on canvas, 28^3/$_4$"×23^5/$_8$"
Antwerp, Carlo van den Bosch collection

Marcel Duchamp

Born, 1887, at Blainville, in Normandy, the youngest of three very gifted brothers, the other two being Jacques Villon and Raymond Duchamp-Villon. Studied at the Académie Julian in Paris, and was also trained as a librarian. In 1913 he went to New York, and took part in the great Armory Show. With Picabia and Man Ray he started a movement which in some respects anticipated the Dadaist movement in Europe. After the first war he returned to Paris, where he was active in the Surrealist movement till 1925, when he settled finally in New York and gave up all artistic work. Duchamp is the inventor of 'ready-mades', mechanical objects which, deflected from their normal use, take on a new existence from their strange and incongruous setting *(Cocoa-mill.)* From this originated a new dream-world full of shocks and contradictions.
Originally a Cubist, Duchamp came to occupy a special place of his own, for his painting contains both the static elements of Cubism and the dynamic elements of Futurism; at the same time he was a forerunner of Surrealism.

80. Transition from virgin to bride 1912   *p. 138*
Oil on canvas, 23^1/$_2$"×21^1/$_4$". Signed and dated centre base: "Marcel Duchamp 1912", on the left: "Le Passage de la Vierge à la Mariée"
New York, Mme. P. Matisse collection

81. Cocoa-mill No. 2 1914   *p. 139*
Oil on canvas. Title and date at base on left: "Broyeuse de Chocolat 1914"
Philadelphia, Philadelphia Museum of Art. (Louise and Walter Arensberg collection)

82. Réseaux de stoppages-étalon 1914   *p. 139*
Oil on canvas, 55^1/$_8$"×39^3/$_8$"
New York, Mme. P. Matisse collection

Raymond Duchamp-Villon

Born at Damville in Normandy in 1876, the second of three gifted brothers (see above). He studied medicine and only began sculpture in 1898. At first he came under Rodin's influence, and later under that of his brothers, Jacques Villon and Marcel Duchamp. It was not till he came in contact with the Cubists and Apollinaire's circle that he began to go his own way and find a style for himself. Between 1912 and 1914 he worked on a series of variations of *The Horse (Le Cheval),* which became a sort of manifesto of Cubist sculpture. He died at Cannes in 1918.
Duchamp-Villon distorts his subject without being an Expressionist. The movement in space so dear to Futurists (as in the motifs *The Horse*) excites him in the same way as it excites Boccioni. His restrained work shows a clear and sturdy intellect, which expresses itself in a style of sober grandeur.

83. The Horse 1914   *p. 248*
Bronze, Ht. 39^3/$_8$", Wdth. 43^1/$_4$", Dpth. 43^1/$_4$"
Paris, National Museum of Modern Art

Raoul Dufy

Born at Le Havre in 1877. Being one of a large family in modest circumstances, he was obliged to go out to work in his youth, though at the same time he attended evening classes at the Ecole des Beaux-Arts. In 1900 he was awarded a scholarship which enabled him to work in Paris where he studied in Bonnat's class in the Ecole des Beaux-Arts. He was deeply interested in the Impressionists and Post-Impressionists, drew in the manner of Toulouse-Lautrec and painted in the manner of Picasso, but he managed to avoid their disintegration of form. About 1905 he turned to Fauvism and met Braque who introduced him to Cézanne's work. This led him to study the structure of trees and living creatures. About 1910 a visit to Orgeville gave added impetus to his study of structure, and the sight of the stained-glass windows of the Cathedral of Evreux helped him to enrich his palette. Beset by financial difficulties he turned towards the graphic arts and executed a large number of woodcuts influenced by folk art. Between 1911 and 1914, encouraged by the couturier Poiret, he started textile-designing. In 1919, inspired by a visit to Vence, he began to use brighter colour; his drawing became more relaxed and developed towards a sort of Baroque ornateness. He abandoned woodcuts for lithography. In 1921 he held his first exhibition at the Bernheim-Jeune galleries. His art became more and more dynamic, his line and colour more sensitive. He adopted watercolour as another means of expression. Travelled much in Italy, Belgium and Morocco. From 1940 to 1950 he lived in Perpignan. About 1944, influenced by music, which inspired his series of *Orchestras*, he turned to 'tonal' painting. Exhibitions and critical examinations of his work followed one another in swift succession. At the Venice Biennale in 1952 he was awarded the *Grand Prix* for painting. He died in Forcalquier in 1953.

84. *The country dance at Falaise* 1906   *p. 102*
Oil on canvas, $30^1/_8'' \times 33^5/_8''$. Signed and dated at base on left: "Raoul Dufy 1906"
Paris, private collection

85. *The bather* 1914   *p. 102*
Oil on canvas, $96^1/_2'' \times 71^5/_8''$
Scheveningen, Mrs. Roëll-Jas' collection

86. *La Baie des Anges* 1927   *p. 103*
Oil on canvas, $31^7/_8'' \times 39^3/_8''$. Signed centre base: "Raoul Dufy"
Brussels, Philippe Dotremont collection

87. *Artist and his model in the studio at Le Havre* 1929   *p. 48*
Oil on canvas, $39^3/_8'' \times 47^1/_4''$. Signed and dated centre base with inscription: "A messieurs Josse et Gaston Bernheim. Raoul Dufy"
Paris, Bernheim-Jeune-Dauberville

James Ensor

Born at Ostend in 1860 of a Flemish mother and an English father. As a child he loved to be in his grandmother's shop, in which she sold masks, boxes ornamented with shells, and Oriental knick-knacks. Studied in the Brussels Académie des Beaux-Arts. Began painting under the aegis of the Belgian print-maker and painter, Félicien Rops. In 1888 Ensor produced *The entry of Christ into Brussels* which aroused widespread interest by virtue of its technique and its revolutionary handling of figures, and anticipated Fauvism and Expressionism. Ensor was one of the founders of *Les XX* and of *L'Art Contemporain*. He was a complete artist who created his own universe side by side with the world of reality.

After a sombre Impressionist period of deep colours, he moved into a *période claire*, characterised by a freer technique and more radiant colour. But although he drew his inspiration from reality, his exceptional talents are shown most clearly in the fantastic visions in which skeletons and masks become symbols of human passions and human vice. Ensor gave a new impetus to Belgian 19th century painting. He was a great pioneer and his technical innovations opened the road to Expressionism, while his fantastic works are precursors of Surrealism.

88. *The entry of Christ into Brussels* 1888   *p. 80–81*
Oil on canvas, $101^5/_8'' \times 169^5/_8''$. Signed and dated at the base towards the right: "J. Ensor. 1888"
London, Louis Franck collection (on loan to the Royal Museum of Fine Arts, Antwerp)

89. *Skeletons warming themselves* 1889   *p. 82*
Oil on canvas, $29^1/_2'' \times 23^5/_8''$. Signed and dated at base on left: "Ensor 89"
Fort Worth, Texas, Robert F. Windfohr

Max Ernst

Born in 1891 at Brühl in the Rhineland. The son of an amateur painter, he studied philosophy at Bonn University. As a painter he was self-taught. His first exhibition was in Berlin in 1913. From 1919 he took part in the Dada movement, started in Zurich in 1916. In 1920 he exhibited his first collages which greatly influenced surrealist ideas. Settled in Paris in 1922 and became one of the promoters of Surrealism. From 1941 to 1945 he was living in New York, then moved to Sedona, Arizona. Married Dorothy Tanning, the American painter. In 1954 he won the Grand Prix at the Venice Biennale. Now living in France.

His work derives its grandeur from his inexhaustible imagination, which enables him to delve into the mysteries of nature and the human subconscious, to create a world which is at the same time natural and fantastic.

90. *The elephant Celebes* 1921   *p. 40*
Oil on canvas, $48^7/_8'' \times 42^1/_8''$. Inscribed at base on right: "Celebes"
London, Roland Penrose collection

91. *A time of stillness* 1939   *p. 184*
Oil on canvas, $66^7/_8'' \times 128''$. Signed at base on right: "Max Ernst"
In the artist's possession

Lyonel Feininger

Born in New York of German parents in 1871, his father being a violinist, his mother a singer. He was himself very gifted musically. In 1887 the family settled in Germany. Giving up his musical studies to concentrate on painting, he attended courses in Hamburg and later in Berlin. Contributed drawings to American and German reviews. Made several visits to Paris, where, in 1911 he got in touch with Delaunay and the Cubists. In 1913 he contributed to the *Blaue Reiter* exhibition in Berlin. In 1919 he was the first artist invited by Gropius, the architect, to teach at the Bauhaus at Weimar, where he was joined by Klee and Kandinsky. All of them were dismissed when the Bauhaus was closed down by the Nazis in 1933. Feininger and three others, Klee, Kandinsky, and Jawlensky, formed a group known as *Die blauen Vier*. In 1937 he left Germany for political reasons and settled in New York, where he died in 1956.

Before the first war, Feininger had already adopted a geometrical style which later became accentuated under the influence of Cubism. His paintings of buildings and ships no less than his landscapes were made radiant with light reflected by or refracted into subtly coloured surfaces. In that way he created the impression of pure and unreal space which characterised his work.

92. *The east choir of Halle cathedral* 1931   *p. 134*
Oil on canvas, $39^3/_8'' \times 31^1/_2''$
Hamburg, Art Museum

Emil Filla

Born in 1882 at Chropyne, Czechoslovakia. Studied art for a while in Prague, but was for the most part self-taught. At Prague he joined the *Groupe des 8*, whose aim was to give a new direction to Czech art. After 1911 Filla turned away from the Expressionist style he had so far employed. Under the influence of Braque and Picasso he espoused analytical Cubism. From 1911 to 1914 he played an active part in the *Manès* group. Worked in Holland from 1914 to 1919. Until 1940 he painted large, figurative scenes inspired by folk songs, legends, and the struggles of his people, some of which were prophetic of the war to come. From 1940 he was held as a hostage at Mauthausen. In the last years of his life he produced a vast cycle of landscapes. He died in Prague in 1953.

93. *Black mandolin 1933*   *p. 120*
Oil on canvas, $25^1/_4'' \times 34^1/_4''$. Signed and dated, centre base:
"Emil Filla 1933"
Private collection

Kai Fjell

Born in 1907 at Sköger in Norway, and started drawing when still a child. He was encouraged by his teacher Nilo Schjelbred, a friend of Edward Munch. In 1930 he went to Oslo where he designed posters and did other decorative work. Then he settled near Telemark to devote himself to painting. For a while in 1932 he studied at the Academy. He travelled abroad occasionally, but made no effort to get in touch with other artists. He was thus practically uninfluenced by modern European movements. He was one of the young Norwegian artists who, between the wars, were developing a personal style based on Nordic traditions and romanticism, but in direct contact with reality and life.

94. *The musician 1937*   *p. 96*
Oil on canvas, $47^1/_4'' \times 55^1/_8''$. Signed and dated at base on
right: "Fjell, 37"
Oslo, Mrs. A. Platon collection

Sam Francis

Born at San Mateo, California, in 1923. Studied medicine and psychology at the University of California. Served as a soldier during the war, was wounded, and began to take an interest in art during his time in hospital. In 1947 he produced his first abstract paintings.
In 1950 Francis received his M. A. and went to Paris, where he now lives. Between 1956 and 1958 he worked on large murals for the Basle *Kunsthalle*, and in 1957 he did murals for the school for flower arrangement at Sofu, Tokyo. Francis' canvasses, frequently large, exude a quiet calm. The resultant expression is one of quiet strength, though accented by warm modulations, sometimes light, sometimes dark. Francis strives in his painting towards the objectivisation of inner life. That is what distinguishes him from other Tachistes and experimenters who draw on the subconscious.

95. *Summer No. 1 1957*   *p. 221*
Oil on canvas, $103^7/_8'' \times 78''$
New York, Martha Jackson Gallery

Naum Gabo

Born at Briansk on the Caspian in 1890. Studied medicine and physics at Munich (1909). He soon made contact with artistic circles, however, and met Kandinsky. From 1913

to 1914 he stayed in Paris with his brother, the sculptor Antoine Pevsner. He then studied art at Oslo, where he produced his first sculptures in a style of geometrical Cubism. In 1917 the two brothers returned to Russia, intending to undertake a radical reform of art. But their Constructivist principles (Manifesto of 1920) were out of step with the cultural and artistic policy of Communism, and in 1921 they had to leave the country. Gabo settled in Berlin, but in 1933 he had to flee once again. He took refuge in London, eventually moving to America, where he is still working.
Gabo propounds the thesis that art is a social force. Therefore, he seeks to free sculpture from the expressions of subjective emotions and traditional materials. He works for preference in transparent substances. His compositions are three-dimensional equations in which light and movement blend in a clear, harmonious rhythm.

96. *Translucid bronze 1953*   *p. 271*
Phosphorus and bronze, Ht. $27^5/_8''$
In the artist's possession

97. *Construction in space 1953*   *p. 270*
Plastic and metal, Ht. 63''
In the artist's possession

Pablo Gargallo

Born at Maella in Spain in 1881. Studied at Barcelona. Won a scholarship which enabled him to go to Paris in 1906 and continue his studies there. In 1917 he returned to Spain and became a professor at the Academy of Barcelona. In 1924 he again spent some time working in Paris. He died in Spain in 1934.
Gargallo was a sculptor who expressed himself chiefly in metals. His style is allied to Archipenko's Cubism, but, in line with Spanish taste, it is more baroque. His figures, made up of convex or concave forms, give an illusion of volume by the use of the same technique as that employed by Gonzalez and Zadkine.

98. *Prophet's head*   *p. 251*
Bronze, Ht. $12^5/_8''$
Madrid, Museum of Modern Art

Paul Gauguin

Born in 1848 in Paris, but brought up at Lima in Peru. Went to sea at 16, but later became a bank clerk in Paris. He began to paint as an amateur, presently throwing up his job and embarking on the precarious life of an artist. He met the Impressionists, and Pissarro who gave him some advice. In 1888 he was joined by other young artists at Pont-Aven in Brittany, where the friendships he made were dominated by his strong personality. After a short stay in Paris he decided to leave Europe altogether, and he sailed for Tahiti in 1891. Later he moved to the Marquesas Islands. In 1903 he died on one of them, Hiva-oa, as a result of disease and privations.
After an Impressionist period, Gauguin, under the influence of Cézanne, found his own style, a reaction against Impressionism. The colour is pure, and the synthetist outline plays a large part in the composition. In the South Seas he created a figurative world based on new relationships between form and colour. As a sculptor Gauguin rejected every academic formula, taking as his point of departure popular Breton or exotic art.

99. *The king's wife (Woman with mangoes) 1896*   *p. 86*
Oil on canvas, $38^1/_8'' \times 51^1/_8''$. Signed and dated at base on

right: "P. Gauguin 1896". Inscription at base on right: Te
Aru Vahine
Moscow, Pushkin Museum

100. The ford 1901   p. 87
Oil on canvas, 28³|₄"×36¹|₄". Signed and dated at base
towards the right: "Paul Gauguin 1901"
Moscow, Pushkin Museum

Ivan Generalic

Born in Hlebine, a Croatian village, in 1914. A self-taught
painter. In 1929 he met Hegedusic who gave him encouragement and advice. In his native village a group of
peasant-painters gathered round him, calling themselves
the Hlebine School, and they have become the most important group of popular artists in Yugoslavia today. None
have had an academic training, their style being derived
from local folk tradition. Composition and execution are
simple and direct. His pictures, often scenes of peasant life,
are frequently done on glass; he is an expert in that field.
He still lives at Hlebine.

101. Burial of Stef Halacek 1934   p. 60
Oil on canvas, 19⁵|₈"×18¹|₂". Monogrammed at base on left:
"I. G."
Zagreb, Modern Art Gallery of the Yugoslav Academy of
Arts and Sciences

102. Beneath the pear tree 1943   p. 193
Oil on canvas, 15³|₄"×19⁵|₈"
Zagreb, Modern Art Gallery of the Yugoslav Academy of Arts
and Sciences

Nicolas Ghika

Born in Athens in 1906. Was a pupil of the artist Parthenis
until 1922, when he went to Paris and studied under
Bissière at the Académie Ranson. Learnt print-making from
his countryman Galanis. Ghika has designed scenery, also
masks and costumes both for ballet and theatre. In 1950
he contributed to the Venice Biennale. Lives in Athens.
His work is inspired by the folk art and folklore of his
country.

103. Shooting-gallery 1952   p. 195
Oil on canvas, 94¹|₂"×78³|₄". Signed and dated at base on
right: "Ghika 52"
In the artist's possession

Alberto Giacometti

Born in 1901 at Stampa in the Italian part of Switzerland,
the son of an Impressionist landscape painter. Studied in
Geneva and later in Rome. His first sculptures-objets date
from 1925–1928. About 1930 he was, for a short period,
drawn towards Surrealism, and he also wrote poems. From
1935 the human form took a predominant place in his
work. Expressionist in form, Surrealist in spirit, his long,
thin figures take on the magic of primitive sculpture, and
we find the same quality also in his drawings, which form
an important part of his work.

104. The invisible object 1935   p. 258
Black bronze, Ht. 61", Wdth. 12⁵|₈"
Paris, Aimé Maeght collection

105. Tall figurine 1957   p. 258
Bronze, Ht. 78³|₄"
Paris, Aimé Maeght collection

Vincent Van Gogh

Born at Groot-Zundert in Holland in 1853. After un-
successful ventures as a picture-dealer and as a master in
an English boarding-school, he decided to follow in his
father's footsteps as a preacher. For a while de did missio-
nary work in a Belgian mining district, but this too was
a failure. In 1880 he began to draw and paint and in so
doing discovered his true vocation. After a period in Holland (Etten, The Hague, Drenthe, Nuenen), he went in
1885 to Antwerp, moving the following year to Paris,
where he found his brother, Theo, who was to sustain
and support him for the rest of his life. He got in touch
with the Impressionists, with Seurat and Signac. In 1888
he left Paris for Arles where he was joined by Gauguin.
Van Gogh's psychological balance was already precarious,
and these two artists did not get on well together. In May
1889 Van Gogh entered the asylum at Saint-Rémy, where
he stayed a year. In May 1890 he went to Auvers-sur-Oise,
where he was under the care of Dr. Gachet. In July of
the same year he committed suicide.
Van Gogh was the first deliberately to exploit distortion
in the service of Expressionism. He turned his back on all
that was conventional and academic, seeking his inspiration in the living sources of human existence. Colour and
form became the means of expression of this painter who,
unlike the Impressionists, gave first place to the human
factor. In his work, ethical elements (Millet) and pictorial
elements (Delacroix and the Impressionists) were absorbed in a new synthesis. Van Gogh's work was ahead of
its time and was destined to exert a great influence on the
Fauves and the Expressionists, to say nothing of his extraordinary example to the 20th century as an intensely
creative personality.

106. Montmartre 1887   p. 77
Oil on canvas, 37³|₄"×47¹|₄"
Amsterdam, Stedelijk Museum

107. Vincent's house at Arles 1888   p. 76
Watercolour and pen, 9⁵|₈"×12"
Amsterdam, V. W. van Gogh
(on loan to the Stedelijk Museum, Amsterdam)

108. Portrait of Armand Roulin 1888   p. 78
Oil on canvas, 25⁵|₈"×21¹|₄"
Essen, Folkwang Museum

109. The prison court-yard 1890   p. 79
Oil on canvas, 31¹|₂"×25¹|₄"
Moscow, Pushkin Museum

Nathalie Gontcharova

Born in 1881 in a country house, 'Ladygine', in the Tula
province south of Moscow. Her great-grandmother had
been Pushkin's wife. Goncharova read science in Moscow,
then in 1898 studied sculpture under Paul Troubetzkoy at

the Academy. Completed her education by travelling widely in Russia and Western Europe. From 1904 she devoted herself entirely to painting and in 1910 turned to abstract art. Allied herself to Larionov in the defence of Rayonism. Designed ballet costumes and Constructivist theatre sets. For Diaghilev she designed many sets, including one for Rimsky Korsakov's *Coq d'Or*. Since 1914 she has lived in Paris.

In spite of all the influence exerted upon her in France, her work remains typically Russian. It offers a Russian solution to the problems raised by abstract art in its attempt to make use of light as an element of painting.

110. Woman weaving   1910   *p. 132*
Oil on canvas, 63" × 46¹/₂"
In the artist's possession

Julio Gonzalez

Born in Barcelona in 1876 into a family of goldsmiths. He and his brother learned the art of working in metal early in life in their father's workrooms. Their father was also a sculptor. Later they studied painting at the Art School in Barcelona. About 1900 the Gonzalez family moved to Paris where Julio met Picasso and joined his group. He drew and did pastels which were strongly influenced by Degas and Puvis de Chavannes. He also did his first sculptures at that time. After his brother's death he continued to sculpt, beset by material and mental worries and in almost total solitude. In 1927 he found his true bent and executed his first sculptures in punched wrought iron. He also freed himself from the Cubist influence and worked on a series of figures in iron and bronze. Despite some of his works, Gonzalez is not an abstract sculptor; he derived his inspiration from the study of nature. He died in Arcueil in 1942.

111. Woman with mirror   1937   *p. 67*
Iron, Ht. 80³/₄"
Paris, private collection

112. La Montserrat   1937   *p. 254*
Iron, Ht. 65"
Amsterdam, Stedelijk Museum

Arshile Gorky

Born in 1905 at Khorkom Vari in Turkey, where he spent his childhood. A self-taught painter. The wild and mountainous scenery of his country and the songs and dances of the Armenian people had a strong influence on his art. In 1920 he settled in America and studied the masters – both ancient and modern – in the galleries there. His first works showed the influence of Cézanne, Picasso, Kandinsky, and above all Miró. About 1930 he began experimenting in abstract art, first as a Cubist, later in freer and non-figurative form. Many of his works were inspired by landscapes. Images taken from nature – consciously or subconsciously – emerge transposed into visual, half-abstract symbols, Surrealist in character. Gorky has a great feeling for his material; his work is poetic, warm in colour, the expression of a passionate and tragic life. He killed himself in 1949.

Gorky was a pioneer of the second group of abstract artists in America, and in the last years of his life he played an important part in the Abstract-Expressionist movement.

113. Betrothal (II)   1947   *p. 191*
Oil on canvas, 45¹/₄" × 34¹/₂"
New York, Whitney Museum of American Art

Morris Graves

Born in 1910 at Fox Valley, Oregon, but in 1911 the family moved north into Washington. At the age of 18 he left school and started travelling. He went to Japan, and later to France and Mexico. In 1946, with a grant from the Guggenheim Foundation, he went back to the East and worked for some months at Honolulu. He was greatly influenced by the works of art he studied in eastern collections. In 1954 he went to Japan for the third time, then stayed for a while in Ireland. Now living at Edmonds, Washington.

Graves continues the line of romantics who flourished in 19th century America. Influenced by the oriental mentality, he looks on art as the expression of an inner force or religious feeling. His style was considerably influenced by the revelation in the thirties of Mark Tobey's 'white writing', based on the technique of Chinese painting. Graves's art is lyrical and fantastic, sometimes inspired by the wild scenery of the Rockies.

114. Fish in sea and stars   1944   *p. 235*
Distemper, 18⁷/₈" × 53¹/₂"
Seattle Art Museum (gift of Mrs. Thomas D. Stimson)

Emilio Greco

Born in 1913 at Catania in Sicily. He began to paint when young, and learned the elements of sculpture in the workshop of a local stonemason. During his military service, he managed to put in some time at the art school in Palermo. In 1945 he settled in Rome, where he gave his first exhibition in 1946. He now teaches in the art school of Naples.

At Rome Greco was influenced by Marini and by Hellenism. He did heads and torsos. In recent years he has undertaken more imposing figures, working always with a graceful touch which reminds one of Mascherini's, though Greco's forms are always more supple, in the manner of the *Serpentinata* of the 16th century, and are charming in their stylised sensuality.

115. Girl bathing No. 2   1957   *p. 263*
Bronze, Ht. 66⁷/₈"
In the artist's possession

Juan Gris (José Gonzalez)

Son of a merchant, Gris was born in Madrid in 1887. Though destined originally for a technical career, he went to Paris in 1906 to devote himself entirely to painting. He rapidly won his way into the advanced circles in which Picasso was already a leading figure and in which Cubism was the order of the day. Juan Gris was handicapped by delicate health. In 1920 he went down with tuberculosis, but he nevertheless managed to go on working, his talents manifesting themselves in several fields. He did some work for Diaghilev's ballets at Monte Carlo and some lithographs for book-illustration. He also gave lectures in support of his artistic beliefs. He died at Boulogne-sur-Seine, near Paris, in 1927.

His work, created under the influence of a group which included Braque, Picasso, and Lipchitz, the sculptor, had nevertheless a style of its own, characterised by sobriety and refinement. His cubism was more figurative than abstract. Beginning with 'form', he eventually reached the 'object', his idea being, in his own words, to put the abstract into concrete form. Equilibrium and refinement are matched by an extraordinary clarity, more intellectual than sensuous. Gris' importance was never fully recognised during his lifetime.

116. Still-life with lamp   1919   *p. 115*
Oil on canvas, $25^5/_8'' \times 31^5/_8''$. Signed and dated top left:
"Juan Gris 12–19"
Otterlo, Kröller-Müller Rijksmuseum

117. The electric lamp   1925   *p. 116*
Oil on canvas, $25^5/_8'' \times 31^7/_8''$
Paris, Louise Leiris Gallery

Marcel Gromaire

Born at Moyelles-sur-Sambre in the north of France in 1892, his father being French, his mother Flemish. A self-taught painter. Frequenting the studios of Montparnasse, he made friends with pupils of Matisse. Served in the first war and was wounded in 1916. After the war, under Léger's influence, he developed a monumentalistic-Expressionist style. In 1937 he decorated the Sèvres Pavilion at the Exposition Universelle in Paris, and also did cartoons for tapestries. Since 1939 he has been working with Lurçat for the Aubusson works. In 1952 he won the Carnegie Prize.

Gromaire belongs wholeheartedly to the Expressionist movement. He is interested in social problems and in the lives of peasants and workmen. Tired of Cubist still-lifes, he brings fresh themes into his paintings, often scenes of ordinary life, but he has retained the Cubist's strict structural principles. Monumental in style, with sombre, bitter colouring, his works are not lacking in decorative grandeur. They are reminiscent of fresco technique, and are thus admirably suited to tapestries, the modern revival of which owes much to him.

118. War   1925   *p. 157*
Oil on canvas, $51^1/_8'' \times 37''$. Signed and dated at base on right:
"Gromaire 1925"
Paris, Petit Palais

Georges Grosz

Born in Berlin in 1893. Studied at Dresden and at his native town. Worked at first as a caricaturist for satirical reviews. After the first war he joined the Dadaists. In 1925 he allied himself briefly with the *Neue Sachlichkeit* movement. Went to New York in 1932 and settled in the United States the following year, becoming naturalised five years later. Lives at Huntington, Long Island.

Grosz is one of the artists who came of age during the first war and seek to exploit the principles of Expressionism in the furtherance of their political views. In his engravings he is usually attacking the decadence of the urban middle classes. With persistent violence he impugns the human animal and his egotism, and his anti-aesthetic attitude makes his art all the more merciless. His style, based on an expressive realism, still has some points of contact with the

Neue Sachlichkeit movement, but also contains some elements of Surrealism.

119. Homage to Oskar Panizza (Nightmare)   1917/1918
$55^1/_8'' \times 43^1/_4''$ *p. 164*
Stuttgart, State Gallery

Alexandre Mikhailovitch Guerassimov

Born at Mitchurinsk in Russia in 1881. Studied in Moscow at the School of Fine Art. Has contributed to many important exhibitions in Russia, East Germany, Hungary, India, China, Finland, the 17th Venice Biennale, the Paris Exposition Universelle, and the New York World Fair. Lives in Moscow.

120. Portrait of Guedike   1956   *p. 201*
Oil on canvas, $57^1/_8'' \times 48^3/_8''$
Property of the U.S.S.R.

Otto Gutfreund

Born at Dvur Králové in northern Bohemia in 1889. Studied in Prague, and in 1909–1910 worked in Paris with Bourdelle. Travelled in England, Holland, and Germany, then settled in France, remaining there throughout the first war. By 1911 he was already applying the principles of analytical Cubism to sculpture. After the first war he moved towards a Realist style with classical tendencies. He then came under the influence of Egyptian sculpture and some of the polychrome sculpture of the Italian Renaissance, and tried new experiments in a series of monumental statues. He became increasingly interested in social problems. His career was brought to an abrupt end by his tragic death in Prague in 1927. Gutfreund is credited with the revival of sculpture in Czechoslovakia.

121. Woman's head   1919   *p. 251*
Bronze, Ht. $10^3/_4''$
Private collection

Renato Guttuso

Born at Bagheria in Sicily in 1912. As a boy he loved to loiter in the workshops in which the peasants' carts were painted. Studied law in Sicily, but broke off in 1931 when he went to Naples and then to Milan. He was one of the founders of the *Fronte nuovo delle Arti*, a group engaged in combating 19th century academism. Author of essays and articles. Lives in Rome.

After his Expressionist beginnings, followed by the influence of Picasso, Guttuso produced his first Neo-Realist work in 1937. His themes are taken from social and political questions. Painted in a violently realistic style, his pictures give a commentary on contemporary manners.

122. Boy on a boat   1956   *p. 197*
Oil on canvas, $38^5/_8'' \times 53^1/_8''$
Milan, Angelo Gussoni collection

Hans Hartung

Born at Leipzig in 1904. After a period in Basle, he lived in Dresden till 1932. Began to paint and draw at an early age, interesting himself chiefly in the work of Kokoschka, Nolde, and Marc. Studied philosophy and history of art in Munich where he met Kandinsky. Paid several visits to Paris between 1925 and 1930. His first exhibition was in Dresden in 1931. He left Germany for Paris in 1935. Served during the war in the Foreign Legion, and became naturalised in 1946.

Strictly speaking, Hartung's work is never realistic. His post-war abstract paintings show great imaginative power and belong to no particular school. His sensitive, dynamic forms almost approach the abstract, while still leaving the object or theme identifiable. An important and independent figure in the generation after Picasso.

123. *T 1956-9*   *p. 53*
Oil on canvas 71"× 54"
Paris, private collection

Karl Hartung

Born in 1908 in Hamburg, where he studied applied art. Lived in Paris from 1929 to 1932, then spent a year in Florence. After that he lived in Hamburg till 1936, when he moved to Berlin, where he still lives today and where he is now teaching at the Hochschule für Bildende Künste. He started on non-figurative work in 1933, but under the Nazi oppression he was unable to exhibit till after the war.

Though isolated, Karl Hartung was able to develop a very individual, expressive style. He sometimes tends towards the figurative, though reducing it, like the Cubists, to its elements. At other times he produces forms which are purely imaginative. In some works these two tendencies are intimately blended. These are often static objects in which, as in the example illustrated, the relationship between the form and the intermediate space endows them with great power. With his versatility and imaginative power, Karl Hartung is in the front rank of present-day German sculptors.

124. *Sculpture 1956*   *p. 284*
Bronze, Ht. 23⁵⁄₈"
Private collection

Erich Heckel

Born in 1883 at Döbeln in Saxony, Heckel studied architecture at Dresden, but is self-taught with regard to painting. After a while he abandoned architecture to devote himself entirely to painting. In 1909 he travelled in Italy. As a soldier during the first war, he met James Ensor and Max Beckmann in Flanders. Lived in Berlin from 1918 till 1944, when he fled to Hemmenhofen on Lake Constance, where he still lives. In 1949 he was given a teaching post at the Academy in Karlsruhe.

With Kirchner and Schmidt he was one of the founders of *Die Brücke*. Other artists joined later. They were the active promoters of Expressionism in Germany. From the first, all Heckel's interest was concentrated on the content of the work. His paintings, prints, and drawings express a revulsion and above all a sharing of the sufferings of the ordinary man. His lyrical and expressive style is less impulsive and violent than that of the other members of the group.

125. *Spring in Flanders 1916*   *p. 161*
Oil on canvas, 32⁵⁄₈"×37³⁄₄". Signed at base on right:
"Heckel"
Hagen, Karl Ernst Osthaus Museum

Krsto Hegedusic

Born at Petrinja in Croatia in 1901. Studied at Zagreb and then in Paris. Professor at the Zagreb Academy of Art and member of the Zagreb Academy of Science. With other Croatian artists he formed the *Zemlja* group (the word means 'earth') whose object was to bring into being a social art, using new forms. His concise and meticulously observed works show the presence of both Expressionist and Surrealist elements. In the village of Hlebine he discovered the young painter Generalic and other peasant-painters to whom he gave encouragement.

126. *Floods 1932*   *p. 193*
Tempera, oil on canvas, 51⁵⁄₈"×63³⁄₈". Signed and dated at base on right: "K. Heg. 1932"
Zagreb, Modern Art Gallery of Yugoslav Academy of Arts and Sciences

127. *Waters of death 1956*   *p. 238*
Tempera, oil on canvas, 51⁵⁄₈"×63³⁄₄". Signed and dated at base on left: "K. Heg. 1956"
In the artist's possession

Bernhard Heiliger

Born in 1915 in Stettin. Between 1931 and 1934 he attended the Werkschule. Continued his studies in Berlin. In 1938 he went to Paris and worked there for a year. Since 1945 he has been living in Berlin, where he holds a teaching post. Influenced at first by Henry Moore, he later acquired his own simple, individual style, which reveals a great sensibility. He likes to use amorphous materials like cement and manufactured composites. He is one of the artists who are leading German sculpture towards abstract art without renouncing figurative representation.

128. *Vegetative figure 1955*   *p. 278*
Externit, Ht. 78³⁄₄"
Private collection

Barbara Hepworth

Born at Wakefield in Yorkshire in 1903. As a girl she showed a great love of nature. In 1920 she studied sculpture in the art-school at Leeds and from 1921 to 1924 was at the Royal College of Art, where she met Henry Moore, five years her senior. On a journey to Italy she was greatly impressed by Italian art in general, and by Michelangelo in particular. In 1930 she married the painter Ben Nicholson. In Paris in 1932 she made the acquaintance of Arp, Brancusi, and Picasso. Back in England, she turned towards abstract art under the influence of Mondrian, though she still kept a place for figurative work, in her drawings more than in her sculpture. She is not a pupil of Henry Moore, as she is often reputed to be, though there is an undoubted affinity in their work. Her style is individual. She works for preference in wood, stone, and marble. Since 1936 she has been living at St.Ives, Cornwall.

129. *Curved form (Delphi) 1955*   *p. 273*
Nigerian wood 42¹⁄₈"×31⁷⁄₈"
In the artist's possession

Morris Hirshfield

Born of Jewish parents in Russian Poland in 1872, he was still young when he emigrated to the United States. A tailor by trade, he worked for twenty years in the textile business, then turned to the manufacture of slippers. At the age of 67 he began to paint. In his youth he had done a few wood-engravings. Lived in Brooklyn, New York. Died in 1946.

Hirshfield may be classed with the 'naive' painters. Working as an amateur, directed only by his imagination and a technique of his own, he achieved in his unsophisticated way an unquestionable mastery. His drawing is accurate, his composition decorative. He called himself a Realist, but in fact created an erotico-legendary dream world inspired by Hebrew literature.

130. The artist and his model   1945   p. 192
Oil on canvas, 48" × 39". Signed and dated at base on right: "M. Hirshfield 1945"
New York, Sidney Janis Gallery

Ivon Hitchens

Born in London in 1893. Studied at the St. John's Wood School of Art and the Royal Academy School. In 1922, as a member of the *Seven and Five* group, he organised their first exhibition. After the war, he settled in Sussex. In 1951 he won a prize at the Festival of Britain. In 1953 he painted a large mural for the English Folk Song and Dance Society and in 1956 contributed to the Venice Biennale.

Hitchens is a somewhat solitary figure in present-day British painting. In 1930 he had already given to his conception of space a formal expression which recalls oriental calligraphy, and his free technique is a precursor of Tachism. Like the Cubists, he systematically arranges his form and space in parallel surfaces and adapts the same principles for his landscapes, which become abstract transpositions of a direct visual experience. The carefully studied division of the surface and the spontaneity of the colour give an astonishing feeling of space.

131. Vale and footbridge in Sussex   1956   p. 180
Oil on canvas, 20¹/₄" × 41³/₈"
London, private collection

Ferdinand Hodler

Born in 1853 at Gurzelen near Berne. At the age of 19 he went to Geneva to work under Barthelemy Menn, a pupil of Ingres' and a friend of Corot's. The delicate colouring of his early work was suddenly replaced by a linear style of great severity, recalling Holbein. About 1891 his work underwent another change under the influence of Symbolism. In 1895 he began painting grandiloquent historical and mythological scenes on a large scale, and of these he did a great number. His style is angular and firm, and it exploits a certain parallelism in forms, as in the work illustrated. Towards the end of his life he was painting lakes and landscapes in warmer colours. He died in Geneva in 1918.

Like many Swiss artists, Hodler was swayed by rival influences, with France and Impressionism on the one hand and Germany and the Munich school on the other. In some respects he seems in advance of his day, for in contrast to the impressionistic subject-paintings of 1880, he was already aiming at a more stylised reality. Though his technique was always masterful, his inspiration sometimes failed to keep pace; but his precisely drawn, solid work, an augury of Expressionism, has a lasting value.

132. Eurhythmy   1895   p. 84
Oil on canvas, 65³/₄" × 96¹/₂". Signed and dated at base on right: "Ferd. Hodler 1895"
Berne, Art Gallery

Karl Hofer

Born in 1878 at Karlsruhe, where he studied from 1896 to 1902. Worked under Hans Thoma and studied at the Stuttgart Academy. Stayed for some time in Paris where he discovered the work of Cézanne. Spent five years working in Rome. Made friends with the Reinhart family of Winterthur, through whom he had an opportunity of seeing India, where he stayed from 1909 to 1911. In 1913 he settled in Berlin. Was interned in France during the first war. When it was over he became a Professor at Frankfurt Academy. About 1930 he tried some abstract work but soon went back to the sober and expressive style of his early days. In 1933 he was dismissed and his work stigmatized as 'degenerate'. From 1945 till his death in 1955 he was President of the Berlin Academy.

Though experimenting in various styles, Hofer never broke with tradition. Influenced at first by Cézanne and Hans von Marées, he adopted, from 1919 onwards, a sober classical style characterised by dry, depressing colours and violent contrasts. His works, particularly those with human figures, are a prosaic interpretation of a bitter and disheartening reality.

133. Prisoners   1933   p. 166
Oil on canvas, 61³/₄" × 50". Initialled and dated at base right: "CH 33"
Berlin, Mrs. Karl Hofer collection

Edward Hopper

Born in 1882 at Nyack, New York. Studied in New York under Robert Henri. At the age of 24 he spent a year in Paris but without succumbing to the influence of French painting. Since 1908 his work has undergone practically no change in either style or subject. Has won many prizes, and his works hang in the principal galleries of America. Contributed to the 1952 Venice Biennale. Lives in New York.

Hopper's work carries on an old tradition of American Realism. It has affinities with the *American Scene School* which, about 1920, rediscovered the American landscape and the American people. He paints grey streets and simple scenes of daily life, without, however, straying into regionalism. His aim is to reproduce the atmosphere of a place or a period. The impression his work gives of desolation, abandonment, and waiting is reinforced by the rigorous composition and the interplay of light and shadow.

134. New York movie   1939   p. 200
Oil on canvas, 31" × 40¹/₈"
New York, Museum of Modern Art

Yuichi Inoue

Born in Kyoto in 1916. Started life as a schoolmaster. Took a course of painting at the Shunyokai Institute. In 1942 he studied calligraphy under the famous expert Sokyu Ueda. In 1952 he joined other artists in founding a group of *avant-garde* calligraphers called *Bokujin-kai*. He is a follower of the Zen sect of Buddhists. Some of his work was shown in Europe in a travelling exhibition of Japanese calligraphy. In 1957 he contributed to the Sao Paulo Biennale.

135. Calligraphy: Buddha 1957   p. 223
Brush design, Japanese ink on rice paper 28³/₄" × 55¹/₈"
In the artist's possession

Robert Jacobsen

Born in 1912 in Copenhagen. In 1930 he did some sculpture in wood, and in 1940 began working in stone. During the war he was for a while influenced by Viking art. In 1947 he settled in Paris, where he worked in close contact with the Danish painter Mortensen. Since 1949 he has for the most part produced iron constructions, rigorously abstract in style, but he still works from time to time in stone or marble. Lives in Paris.

In his static, sober spatial constructions Jacobsen aims at an equilibrium and harmony between the space and the metal curves that circumscribe it. He belongs to a group of artists who exploit metal sculpture in the service of abstract art, differing from Gonzalez, with whom it remained figurative.

136. Spatial sculpture 1951   p. 276
Iron, coloured black, Ht. 25⁵/₈″
Brussels, Philippe Dotremont collection

Alexej von Jawlensky

Born in 1864 at Torshok in Russia of an aristocratic family. Was sent to a military school, then to study painting under Ilia Repin in St. Petersburg. In 1896 he was at Munich studying at the same time as Kandinsky in the art-school of Anton Aszbe. In 1905 he stayed in Brittany and in Provence. Was influenced by Cézanne, Van Gogh, and Matisse. In 1901 he founded with Kandinsky the *Neue Künstlervereinigung* in Munich. Spent the war years in Switzerland. In 1921 he settled in Wiesbaden. Became a member of *Die Blauen Vier*, with Klee, Kandinsky, and Feininger, and contributed to their numerous exhibitions. In 1934 he was attacked by arthritis, but he managed to go on painting despite the paralysis of his hands. In the last years of his life he turned back to the religion of his youth, the Greek Orthodox Church. Died in 1941 at Wiesbaden.

Jawlensky's work belongs to the culminating period of Expressionism. He stands out from the other members of the *Blauen Vier* by his fervour and by the extreme Fauvism of his palette which reminds one of Byzantine icons and Russian folk painting. He preferred to paint portraits, particularly those whose expressions betrayed an inner life. At the end he turned towards an abstract and spiritualised Expressionism depicting tragic subjects in sombre colours.

137. Woman in a blue hat 1911   p. 125
Oil on cardboard, 27⁵/₈″ × 17⁵/₈″
München-Gladbach, Civic Museum

Oscar Jespers

Born in 1887 at Antwerp where he studied at the art-school. He admired Minne and Meunier and made friends with Rik Wouters. In 1927 he settled in Brussels, where he is still working. Member of the *Groupe des IX, L'Art Vivant* and *L'Art Contemporain*. Honorary professor at the Institut National Supérieur de l'Architecture et des Arts Décoratifs in Brussels. Has done many sculptures for public buildings.

Starting with Impressionism, it was not long before Jespers, reacting against the academism and conventionalism of the 19th century, sought to bring the problems of composition in sculpture once more into the lime-light. He worked directly on stone, the substance imposing its own

severely architectural form, thus bringing it close to Cubism. In the twenties his style developed towards a vigorous Expressionism. He was the first Belgian sculptor to be moved by the same intellectual preoccupations that were haunting the Expressionist painters of the day. Of recent years he has arrived at a noble simplification of reality using full and powerful curves. As a teacher he has exerted a considerable influence.

138. Monument to the poet Paul van Ostaijen 1930/31
                                        p. 253
Granite, Ht. 27⁵/₈″, Wdth. 70⁷/₈″, Dpth. 23⁵/₈″
Antwerp, Schoonselhof

Asger Jorn

Born in 1914 at Vejrum in Denmark. Went to Paris in 1936 and studied painting in Léger's studio. Worked with Le Corbusier on the 'Temps Nouveaux' pavilion at the Exposition Universelle in 1937. Was one of the founders of the *Cobra* group (Copenhagen, Brussels, Amsterdam). Contributed to the first exhibition of experimental art in Amsterdam in 1949. Spent a long time in Italy. Has also done prints, sculpture, and ceramics, and illustrated some Danish books. Lives partly in Paris, partly in Denmark.

Jorn's art is derived from Expressionism. With sensitive and delicate colouring and with considerable freedom of form, he has translated some of the influences of Munich, Soutine, and Kokoschka into an expressionist-abstract style.

139. Letter to my son 1956/57   p. 232
Oil on canvas, 51¹/₈″ × 76³/₄″. Signed and dated at base on right: "Jorn 1956–57"
Rhode-Saint-Genèse, Albert Niels collection

Wassily Kandinsky

Born in 1866 in Moscow of well-to-do parents. Studied law. It was not till he was thirty that he decided to devote himself to painting. In 1896 he went to Munich, where he and Jawlensky studied at the Aszbe art-school, and at the Akademie der Bildenden Künste. Travelled in France, Italy, and Tunisia. Back in Munich in 1908 he became the leader of the *Neue Künstlervereinigung*. With Franz Marc he published *Der Blaue Reiter*, a title that was later to be adopted by the advanced group of painters who gave their first exhibition in Munich in 1911. In 1912 Kandinsky published a summing-up of his views on art entitled *Über das Geistige in der Kunst*. The revolution in Russia took him back to his country, as it took Chagall, Gabo, and Pevsner. In 1918 he was given a teaching post in Moscow. In 1921 however, new policies on culture forced him to leave the country again, and he was given a post at the Dessau Bauhaus, where he found the climate favourable to the dissemination of his views on art. In 1933, however, he was to be a refugee once again, this time from the Nazis. Going to Paris he settled at Neuilly, where he died in 1944.

Before reaching the realms of purely abstract art, Kandinsky went through a period, lasting from 1906 to 1909, in which his work was illustrative, using stylised forms in simple colours reminiscent of icons and Russian folklore. Between 1910 and 1914, while still producing representative works, he embarked on abstract art, which he expressed with intense feeling and almost oriental colour. After 1914 his work became more severe, and while he was at the Bauhaus (1922–1923) his forms became more consciously Constructivist.

140. *A street at Murnau* 1909/10   p. 123
Oil on canvas, 13^1/$_4$" × 18". Signed at base on right: "Kandinsky"
Private German collection

141. *Composition No. 2* 1910   p. 124
Oil on canvas, 38^1/$_4$ × 51^5/$_8$". Signed and dated at base on right: "Kandinsky 1910"
New York, The Solomon R. Guggenheim Museum

142. *Composition (sketch for large composition)* 1912   p. 206
Oil on canvas, 37^3/$_8$" × 42^1/$_8$". Signed and dated at base on left: "Kandinsky 1912"
Brussels, Philippe Dotremont collection

143. *In blue* 1925   p. 20
Oil on cardboard, 31^1/$_2$" × 43^1/$_4$". Initialled at base on left: "V. K." On back: "W. K. no. 288"
Brussels, Urvater collection

144. *Accompanied contrast No. 613* 1935   p. 213
Oil and sand on canvas, 37^3/$_4$" × 63^3/$_4$". Initialled at base on left: "V. K. 35"
New York, The Solomon R. Guggenheim Museum

Alexandre Pavlovitch Kibalnikov

Born at Orekhovo, Stalingrad, in 1912. Studied in the art-school at Saratov on the Volga. Has contributed to several exhibitions in the Soviet Union, to the 28th Venice Biennale, and to an exhibition in India. He lives in Moscow.

145. *Maiakovsky* 1956   p. 267
Bronze, Ht. 26", Wdth. 13", Dpth. 11"
Collections of the U.S.S.R.

Ernst Ludwig Kirchner

Born in 1880 at Aschaffenburg in Lower Franconia. Studied architecture in Dresden. Lived in Munich during 1903 and 1904 and devoted himself to painting. In 1905, having returned to Dresden, he became one of the founders of *Die Brücke*. From 1907 to 1909 he worked with this group of friends, who, in 1911 moved to Berlin. There it was that Kirchner painted his celebrated and typical pictures, many of which were inspired by city life. In 1914 he joined the army as a volunteer, but in 1916 he was invalided out and sent to a sanatorium, first in Germany, then at Davos in Switzerland. His work at this period was inspired by nature and country life. From 1926 on he painted his series of huge allegorical pictures. Next, under the influence of Picasso, he groped for fresh solutions and moved towards a more severe style. His paintings were confiscated by the Nazis and a number were hung in the exhibition of 'Degenerate Art' in Munich. In 1938, ill and profoundly disheartened, he committed suicide at Wildboden near Frauenkirch.
Kirchner is the most outstanding figure of *Die Brücke*. In him were combined a sensitive feeling for form and expressive dramatic power. The harsh and violent colouring reminds one of Fauvism. He was more influenced, however, by Munch, and he differs from the French masters in putting greater stress on the emotional expression and the symbolic content than on purely visual effects. Street girls and men-about-town and Berlin street scenes emphasize the solitude of man, lost in the great modern city. Kirchner's point of departure is always man and nature, but he rises above their individual aspects. He was the only one of the *Brücke* group whose harrowing painting remained faithful to Expressionism through the various stages of its development.

146. *The artist and his model* 1907   p. 129
Oil on canvas, 59" × 39^3/$_8$"
Hamburg, Art Museum

147. *Five women in the street* 1913   p. 130
Oil on canvas, 47^1/$_4$" × 35^3/$_8$"
Cologne, Wallraf-Richartz Museum

148. *Chalet in the Alps* 1917   p. 163
Oil on canvas, 47^5/$_8$" × 59". Signed at base on right: "Kirchner"
Karlsruhe, State Art Museum

Paul Klee

Born in 1879 of German parents at Munchenbuchsee near Berne. Son of a musician, he began by studying the violin, but later went to Munich to study painting. In 1901 he began travelling in Italy, returning to Munich in 1906. He fell under the influence of his great predecessors, Van Gogh, Cézanne, Matisse, and of his contemporaries, Macke, Marc, Jawlensky, and above all Kandinsky. In 1911 he was admitted to the *Blaue Reiter* group. In 1914 he travelled in North Africa with Marc. During the war he served in the German army. In 1922 he was given a teaching post at the Dessau Bauhaus. In 1925 he contributed to the first Surrealist exhibition in Paris. Exhibited in Germany with Feininger, Kandinsky, and Jawlensky under the title of *Die Blauen Vier*. In 1931 he was appointed to the Düsseldorf Academy, but in 1933, forced by the Nazi regime to leave the country, he went back to Berne. After years of illness, he died in 1940 at Muralto near Locarno.
It is impossible to over-estimate the importance of Paul Klee. Without being either an abstract painter to the same extent as Kandinsky or a representational painter, he stands at the boundary between these two worlds. No artist has so thoroughly and successfully explored his inner self, while at the same time eliminating the vagaries of his own personality. His paintings reflect the world as he experienced it within himself. Klee's work has become an inexhaustible source for modern art, with its concentration of complex forces revealed in innumerable curious pages thick with colour and scrawled all over.

149. *Carpet of memory* 1914   p. 148
Oil on canvas pasted to cardboard, 15^3/$_4$" × 19^3/$_4$". Signed and dated at base on left: "Klee 1914. 193", on the cardboard: "1914. 193 Teppich der Erinnerung"
Berne, Art Museum, Paul Klee endowment

150. *The magic canary* 1920   p. 39
Oil on canvas, 20^1/$_2$" × 16^1/$_2$". Signed and dated at base on right: "Klee 1920. 24"
Brussels, Philippe Dotremont collection

151. *The actor* 1923   p. 149
Oil on wrapping-paper pasted on cardboard 19^3/$_4$" × 10^1/$_2$". Signed and dated, top right "Klee", on the cardboard: "1923.27 Schauspieler"
Berne, private collection F.K.

152. *Sindbad the sailor (battle scene from comic fantasy-opera)*
1923   *p. 148*
Water colour on paper, mounted on cardboard $15'' \times 20^1/_4''$.
Signed centre right "Klee". On the cardboard "1923. 123"
Muttenz, Mrs. T. Durst-Haass collection

153. *Main-roads and byways*   *1929*   *p. 152*
Oil on canvas, $32^5/_8'' \times 26^3/_8''$
Cologne, private collection

154. *Statue in garden*   *1937(9?)*   *p. 150*
Pastel on canvas, $19^5/_8'' \times 16^1/_2''$. Signed top right: "Klee"
Berne, private collection F.K.

155. *Park at Lucerne*   *1938*   *p. 150*
Oil on jute, $39^3/_4'' \times 28''$. Signed top right "Klee". On the
frame: "Park bei Lu"
Berne, Art Museum, Paul Klee endowment

156. *La belle jardinière*   *1939*   *p. 151*
Oil and tempera on jute, $37^3/_4'' \times 28''$. Signed at base on left:
"Klee"
Berne, Art Museum, Paul Klee endowment

157. *Portrait of Gaia*   *1939*   *p. 151*
Oil on cotton pasted to a panel, $38^1/_8'' \times 27^1/_8''$. Signed top
right: "Klee". On the frame: "1939 Y3"
Berne, private collection F.K.

Franz Kline

Born at Wilkes-Barre in Pennsylvania in 1910. Studied
from 1931 to 1935 at Boston University, then till 1938 at
the Heatherly School of Fine Art, London. In the same
year he returned to America, settling in New York. Teaches
at Black Mountain College and at the Pratt Institute,
Brooklyn. Lives in New York.
Kline is one of the most individualistic and important
American abstract painters. Of spontaneous origin, his
work is strongly linear. His palette is generally limited to
grey, black, and white. The composition forms an ideo-
gram of gigantic proportions, and it would appear to have
been influenced by oriental calligraphy.

158. *White forms*   *1955*   *p. 222*
Oil on canvas, $74'' \times 50''$
New York, Philip Johnson collection

Oskar Kokoschka

Born at Pöchlarn in Austria in 1886, he received his
artistic training in Vienna. A leading modern painter at
twenty-five, he also worked in other fields - poetry,
drama and *belles-lettres*. He represented art in an *avant-
garde* group which included the composer, Schoenberg,
and the architect, Loos. In opposition to the supporters
of *Art for Art's Sake*, he has achieved a unique personal
Expressionism which convinces by its intrinsic moral
quality, rather than relying on aesthetic appeal. Was
invited by Herwarth Walden to collaborate with the
Sturm group in Berlin. In a state of visionary exaltation
at this period, he produced work the central theme of
which was his struggle with himself and his own revolutionary passions. He was wounded in the war in 1916.
In 1918 he settled in Dresden where he was called to a
teaching post at the Academy. Between 1924 and 1931
he travelled widely. In 1931 he was in Vienna. In 1934 he
settled for a while in Prague. In 1938 he fled to London

and later became naturalised. Kokoschka's aesthetic and
political reactions to the dramatic events of his time were
now more than ever reflected in his painting.
Since the war he has been teaching regularly at the Salz-
burg summer school. He is at present living at Villeneuve
on Lake Geneva. Thomas Mann called Kokoschka 'a modern creative spirit whose eyes turn him into a visionary'.
But it is his humanity which shines through all his work:
his late ventures in history and mythology (*Prometheus*,
1950, *Thermopylae*, 1954) serve his humanitarian principles
by expressing the essentially timeless quality of human
experience.

159. *Dents du midi*   *1909*   *p. 159*
Oil on canvas, $29^7/_8'' \times 45^5/_8''$. Initialled at base on right:
"O. K."
Zurich, Mrs. M. Feilchenfeldt collection

160. *Double portrait (Oskar Kokoschka and Alma Mahler)*
1912   *p. 23*
Oil on canvas, $39^3/_8'' \times 35^3/_8''$. Initialled at base on left:
"O. K."
Hamburg, Prof. E. Horstmann collection

161. *The power of music*   *1918*   *p. 159*
Oil on canvas, $40^1/_8'' \times 59''$
Eindhoven, Stedelijk van Abbe Museum

162. *Mont Blanc*   *1927*   *p. 163*
Oil on canvas, $35^3/_8'' \times 51^1/_8''$. Initialled at base on left:
"O. K." On the back: "Nov. 1927 Chamonix"
Zurich, Mme. H. Lütjens collection

Sergey Timofeievitch Konenkov

Born in Smolensk in 1874. Studied at the School of Painting, Sculpture and Architecture, in Moscow, and at the
School of Fine Arts. Has contributed to some important
exhibitions in the Soviet Union and abroad, particularly
in China, Indonesia, and India, and to the 16th and 18th
Venice Biennales. Lives in Moscow.

163. *Dostoievsky*   *1933*   *p. 267*
Bronze, Ht. 22", Wdth. $19^5/_8''$, Dpth. $28^3/_4''$
Moscow, Tretiakov Museum

Willem de Kooning

Born in Rotterdam in 1904. Left school at the age of 12
and was apprenticed as a house-painter. At the same time
he went to evening art classes at the Rotterdam art-school,
where he learnt the principles adopted by the *De Stijl*
movement. On a visit to Belgium, he was greatly impressed by the work of the Flemish Expressionists. In 1926
he was working, still as a house-painter and sign-painter,
in the United States. His first abstract work dates from
1934. After the war he began contributing to the Venice
Biennales and to numerous exhibitions in America. In his
most recent work he has swung back to representational
painting in a definitely Expressionist style.
De Kooning and Pollock are the two outstanding figures
in abstract Expressionism in America. This movement,
which began as a reaction against Mondrian and Neo-
plasticism, has exerted a great influence on the younger
generation.

164. *Gotham News*   *1955*   *p. 56*
Oil on canvas, $69'' \times 79''$. Signed top right: "de Kooning"
Buffalo, Allbright Art Gallery

Hermann Kruijder

Born at Lage Vuursche in Holland in 1881, he was trained as a house-painter. For a while he attended the school of arts and crafts at Haarlem and did some stained-glass work in a workshop at Delft. It was not till 1910 that he concentrated on painting. He died at Haarlem in 1955.
If Kruyder's style and colouring belong to Expressionism, the spirit of his work is of quite a different trend. He distorts reality to adapt it to the symbolic world that haunts his subconscious. In his last years his colours became darker and they were laid on with heavy emphasis.

165. Horseman 1933   *p. 174*
Oil on canvas, $42^7/_8'' \times 59''$. Signed at base on right: "H.
Kruyder"
Amsterdam, Stedelijk Museum

Kukryniksy

Collective pseudonym of a group of three artists, founded in 1924, viz:
Kupryanow, Mikhail Vasilyevich, born in 1903 at Tetinchi in the Tartar Soviet Republic.
Krylov, Porphiry Nikitych, born in 1902 at Chelkunovo, Tula.
Sokolov, Nikolai Alexandrovich, born in 1903 in Moscow.
All three studied at the Moscow Art and Technical workshops. They have contributed to important exhibitions in the Soviet Union and abroad (Finland, China, Bulgaria, East Germany, Poland, Indonesia, Hungary, and Syria), also to the 27th Venice Biennale. They live in Moscow.

166. The end 1947/48   *p. 203*
Oil on canvas, $78^3/_4'' \times 98^1/_8''$. Signed and dated at base on left:
"Kukryniksy 47/48"
Moscow, Tretiakov Museum

Frantisek Kupka

Born at Opočno in Northern Bohemia in 1871. Studied at the Academies of Prague and Vienna. He was interested in philosophy and in the French Encyclopedists, and he sometimes took part as a medium in spiritualist *séances.* Made several journeys to Germany, Sweden, Norway, and England. In 1895 he finally settled in Paris, working there as a painter and illustrator. Some of his illustrations, signed Paul Rengard, were for essays on art. In 1910 he produced his first purely abstract work. With Jacques Villon he took part in the activities of the *Section d'Or.* It was not till after the last war that his merits were recognised. In 1946 a big retrospective exhibition of his work was held in Prague, where a Kupka museum was founded. Kupka died at Puteaux, a suburb of Paris, in 1957.
All through his life Kupka was experimenting, groping for an abstract reality composed of perfectly proportioned geometrical forms. Down to 1910 his work was divided between paintings of a political and satirical nature on the one hand and works of increasingly stylised and Constructivist forms. His abstract composition reaches a high degree of purity and equilibrium which sometimes recalls philosophic systems. Apollinaire classes Kupka as one of the painters of *Orphism.* This important painter, with his structural severity and logical intellect, was one of the prophets of abstract art.

167. Architecture philosophique 1913   *p. 117*
Oil on canvas, $56^1/_4'' \times 44^1/_8''$. Signed and dated at base on right: "Kupka 1913"
Paris, Louis Carré Gallery

Joseph Kutter

Born in Luxemburg in 1894. Studied in Germany, chiefly in Munich, where he discovered and was deeply impressed by Expressionism. In 1924, back in his own country, he evolved an individual style, Expressionist in form but affected by purely pictorial preoccupations. In 1930, he painted the picture included here, the first of a long series of such pictures with solidly built human figures on a rich, unctuous background. During his last illness, which lasted five years, he produced some very touching pictures, tragic in their expression, but always well-balanced. He died in 1941.
Like the French painters, Kutter sacrificed everything to the work's pictorial requirements. But his Expressionism, severe in mood and sometimes harrowing, is none the less closer to German than French painting. Sometimes he reminds one of the Flemish painter Permeke. That he should have affinities on several sides is not surprising considering Luxemburg's position as a meeting place of French, German, and Belgian influences. A pioneer of modern art in his own country, Kutter influenced many young artists, often of widely different tendencies.

168. Man with cut finger 1930   *p. 174*
Oil on canvas, $49^1/_4'' \times 39^3/_8''$. Signed and dated at base on right: "Kutter 30"
Paris, National Museum of Modern Art

Noël Roger de La Fresnaye

Born in 1885 at Le Mans of an old and cultured Norman family. In 1903 he began his studies at both the Académie Julian and the Académie Ranson. In 1908 he studied for a time with Sérusier and Maurice Denis. Influenced at first by Cézanne, he was attracted from 1910 to Cubism, though he never actually belonged to the movement. In 1914 he dropped painting to join the army. He was gassed in 1918 and never really recovered, although he went on working in solitude. His illness affected his creative ability, however. His style became simpler and more traditional. He died at Grasse in 1925.
La Fresnaye was influenced by Cubism without accepting it as a basic theory or rigid formula for his own work. He went on painting subjects borrowed from life (*Women bathing,* 1912, *Married life,* 1913) thus bringing realism and movement into his geometrical composition. His modest but well-balanced work, noble and intelligent, consists of landscapes and still-lives as well as some larger paintings with groups of figures (*Conquest of the Air,* 1913).

169. Married life 1913   *p. 117*
Oil on canvas, $37^3/_4'' \times 46^1/_2''$. Signed at base on left: "R. de La Fresnaye"
Minneapolis, Institute of Arts

170. Seated man 1914   *p. 118*
Oil on canvas, $51^5/_8'' \times 64^1/_2''$
Paris, National Museum of Modern Art

Alexandre Ivanovitch Laktionov

Born in Moscow in 1910. Studied at the Schools of Fine Art at Rostov and Leningrad. Has contributed to numerous exhibitions in the Soviet Union and abroad (Finland, Hungary, East Germany, India, China). Lives in Moscow.

171. A Letter from the Front   1947   *p. 202*
Oil on canvas, 88⁵⁄₈″ × 61″
Moscow, Tretiakov Museum

Wifredo Lam

Born in 1902 at Sagua in Cuba. Studied at Havana, Madrid and Paris. Went to live in Spain in 1921, but moved to Paris in 1937, there meeting Picasso and André Breton. Joined the Surrealist movement. In 1941, he stayed for a while in Havana, then visited the United States. At present he is living in Paris.
His paintings, which depict the jungle, totems, etc., have a fairytale atmosphere. Lam rejects the intellectual themes of European Surrealism, replacing them by magical elements borrowed from primitive civilizations and from the the folklore of his own country.

172. Astral harp   1944   *p. 237*
Oil on canvas, 82⁵⁄₈″ × 74³⁄₄″
Brussels, Urvater collection

Henri Laurens

Born in Paris in 1885; started his career as a scene-painter. As a sculptor, he began with realistic work under the influence of Rodin. In 1911 he met Braque and threw in his lot with Cubism, becoming one of the most important sculptors of the movement. He adapted the principles of Cubist paintings and *collages* to his own art, particularly in a series of bas-reliefs of geometrical composition, most of which were still-lifes. From 1930 a tendency to humanization became noticeable in his work, the female figure playing a predominant part. His monumental group, *L'Eau*, was exhibited at the Exposition Universelle in Paris in 1937. He was an excellent draughtsman, and an important part of his work consists of illustrations. In 1954 Laurens won the prize for sculpture at the Sao Paulo Biennale. He died in Paris in 1954.
This sculptor's work lies entirely within the Cubist movement. Laurens remained faithful to his principles even when he produced large female figures in stone or bronze which expressed both a lyrical melody and a noble restraint. Like Picasso and Braque, he gave new life to Greek mythology by the choice of his themes, both in his sculpture and in his illustrative work.

173. The great musician   1938   *p. 250*
Bronze, 78³⁄₄″ × 47¹⁄₄″
Paris, Louise Leiris Gallery

Sara Dmitrievna Lebedeva

Born in St Petersburg in 1892 and studied there in the private studio of L. V. Sherwood and V. V. Kuznetsov. Lebedeva's pictures have been shown at important exhibitions in the Soviet Union and at the 16th, 18th, 19th, and 28th Venice Biennales. She lives in Moscow.

174. V. P. Tchekalov   1938   *p. 265*
Bronze, Ht. 14⁵⁄₈″, Wdth. 7¹⁄₂″, Dpth. 10⁵⁄₈″
Moscow, Tretiakov Museum

Louis Le Brocquey

Born in 1916 in Dublin, and was brought up there. In 1938 he left the family business to devote himself entirely to painting, in which he was self-taught. He is a member of the Society of Industrial Artists and teaches textile design at the Royal College of Art. He has also done mosaics and designs for tapestries. He represented Ireland at the 1956 Venice Biennale. Lives in London.
Le Brocquey is one of the representatives of the romantic tendency in Great Britain. He paints for the most part groups of figures. In his earlier work his favourite theme was the wandering tinkers of Ireland, but he did not treat it in an anecdotal fashion, taking it rather as symbolic of the artist's free and independent life. He has developed an individual style, in which, however, some modern French influences are discernible, to which must be given some of the credit for his harmony of line and delicacy of touch. In his recent work the human figure becomes a magic presence rather than an abstraction of real life.

175. The family   1951   *p. 197*
Oil on canvas, 67³⁄₈″ × 83¹⁄₈″. Signed and dated at base on left: "Le Brocquey 51"
Milan, La Prealpina S.P.A.

Fernand Léger

Born in 1881 at Argentan in Normandy, the son of a stock-breeder. Was apprenticed as draughtsman to an architect but took courses in private art-schools in Paris and at the Ecole des Arts Décoratifs. Was impressed by the work of Cézanne and Matisse, but the first great influence exerted on him was Cubism. He got in contact with the *Section d'Or*. In 1914 he went to the war and, as a sensitive artist, was profoundly affected by it. Was invalided out of the army as a result of poison gas. The paintings dealing with war subjects are vigorously done, representational in spirit, being inspired directly by the world of machines and men. In 1920 he got to know Le Corbusier. He is the author of a film, *Le Ballet Mécanique*, and has done scene-designing and mural painting. Has travelled a great deal, particularly in America, where he spent the war years, 1940–1945. In 1945 he returned to Paris and in the following year he undertook some mosaics for the church of Assy. In 1951 he designed the stained-glass windows for the little church of Audincourt. He died at Gif-sur-Yvette in 1955.
Léger had never been an orthodox adherent of Cubism, nor did he belong to the abstract school. He dealt with the world of things, recreating objects in a highly individual style, (tubular forms that come near to analytical Cubism). The paintings of his last years proclaim his love of life, of mankind in work and play, as in *The Builders*, 1950, and *The grand parade*, 1953, composed of simplified forms with clear, bright colouring. The architectonic quality of his work is best seen in his mural paintings, mosaics, and stained-glass.

176. Soldier with a pipe   1916   *p. 119*
Oil on canvas, 51¹⁄₈″ × 38¹⁄₈″. Signed and dated at base on right: "F. Léger 16"
Brussels, Philippe Dotremont collection

177. The grand parade   1954   *p. 49*
Oil on canvas, 118¹⁄₈″ × 157¹⁄₂″
Paris, Aimé Maeght collection

Wilhelm Lehmbruck

Born in 1881 at Meiderich, near Duisburg, the son of a miner. Studied at the school of applied art in Duisburg and then at the art-school in Düsseldorf. His works of 1910 already show a mastery of his medium. He travelled from time to time in Italy, and was in Paris from 1910 to 1914, after which he settled in Berlin. He spent 1917 in Zürich, then returned to Berlin. He killed himself in 1919.

Primarily a sculptor, Lehmbruck also made numerous drawings and prints. His early work is traditional, in the vein of Hildebrand in Germany and with Maillol and Rodin in France. He was also interested in Naturalism and the social problems dear to Meunier. By 1911 he had acquired an individual style which had some affinity with Minne's Gothic symbolism. His slender, ethereal figures are full of a static repose, subtle and delicate feeling, and deep inward life. His statue *The Kneeling Woman* was regarded by his contemporaries as a work which opened up a new style of Gothic Expressionism.

178. The kneeling woman 1911   *p. 63*
Bronze, Ht. 70¹/₈″
Duisburg, Municipal Museum of Art

Jacques Lipchitz

Born in 1891 at Druskieniki in Lithuania, where his father, a builder, had intended to make an engineer of him. In 1909, however, Lipchitz went to Paris and attended both the Ecole des Beaux-Arts and the Académie Julian. In 1913 he became acquainted with Diego Rivera and Picasso. Later he made friends with Juan Gris. In 1925 he got Le Corbusier to build him a studio at Boulogne-sur-Seine. In 1940 he took refuge in New York. Returning to Paris for a short stay in 1946, he then settled definitely in America, living at Hastings-on-Hudson near New York.

Passing through Cubism, Lipchitz arrived at a style of his own. He never broke away entirely from representational art. Avoiding the danger, inherent in Cubism, of becoming static, he succeeded after a lot of experiment in creating his *sculptures transparentes* which were to have so many imitators. In the place of the Cubists' harlequins and musicians, he found his subjects in the Old Testament and in the metamorphoses of erotic life. Nor was his style uninfluenced by the modern world, for his work often expresses struggle and suffering, as in the *Prometheus* and *The Sacrifice*. The *Madonna* which he did for the Church of Notre-Dame de Liesse at Assy is a synthesis of his religious feelings and his explorations into the world of form and symbol.

179. Woman bathing 1923/25   *p. 66*
Bronze, Ht. 78³/₄″
In the artist's possession

180. The sacrifice 1949/57   *p. 252*
Bronze, Ht. 55¹/₈″
In the artist's possession

Seymour Lipton

Born in 1903 in New York. Went to City College and Columbia University. Taught himself sculpture. Started working in 1932. Has done many statues for official buildings, including chapels at Tulsa, Oklahoma and at Gary, Indiana, and the Inland Steel Building, Chicago. Lipton has taught sculpture at various schools and since 1956 he has been advisor on art education at New York University. A film has been done on his work. He writes for several art reviews.

Organic forms are the basis of Lipton's abstractions. At first he worked in wood. In 1947 he began working with welded steel. Since 1950 he has been mixing steel with other metals. He seeks always to achieve an equilibrium between space and form. His sculptures are either centrifugal, with the material grouped around an empty space which forms the centre, or they are suspended from a point. Lipton is one of the chief representatives of young abstract sculpture in America.

181. Prophet 1956   *p. 286*
White silver on metal, Ht. 97⁵/₈″
In the artist's possession

Peter Lubarda

Born at Ljubotenje in Montenegro in 1907. Studied in Belgrade and Paris, and was much influenced by the Ecole de Paris. He blends the strong lines of the Montenegran landscape with a delicate use of colour. Nature is shown only in its elemental aspects. His painting, which goes beyond the recognisable, belongs really to abstract Expressionism. Lubarda has exerted a considerable influence on the younger generation of Yugoslav artists.

182. Mediterranean 1952   *p. 234*
Oil on canvas, 57¹/₂″ × 44⁷/₈″. Signed and dated at base on right: "Lubarda 1952"
Belgrade, Gallery of Contemporary Art

Jean Lurçat

Born at Bruyères in the Vosges in 1892. In 1911 he became the pupil of Victor Prouvé, the founder of the School of Nancy. Later he went to Paris and became the pupil of the print-maker Bernard Naudin. Wounded in 1914, he returned to civilian life. He started painting again, but was already beginning on tapestry. The first tapestry was done in 1917, and his first exhibition was in Paris in 1922. He travelled a great deal, visiting Africa, Greece, Asia, America, Russia, and China. In 1937 he began his association with the Aubusson works. He went to live at Aubusson in 1939, but in 1945 he moved to Saint-Céré, where he is now working on a great series of tapestries to be entitled *La Joie de Vivre*, which will symbolise the atomic age with its terrors and its hopes.

Lurçat is both a painter and print-maker, but for the last 25 years he has chiefly produced designs for tapestries. It is largely due to him that the art of tapestry has been revived, and he has done much to get such tapestries accepted as a means of decorating modern architecture. In his work he blends a surrealist Expressionism with poetic and visionary elements.

183. Wine-harvest 1956   *p. 205*
Aubusson tapestry, 129⁷/₈″ × 268⁵/₈″
Paris, Association des Peintres-Cartonniers de Tapisseries

August Macke

Born in 1887 at Meschede in Westphalia. Studied art at Düsseldorf. Travelled widely, particularly in Italy, Holland and Belgium. Stayed in London and several times in Paris, where from 1907 onwards he became associated with Impressionism, Fauvism, and Cubism. For a time he was a pupil of Lovis Corinth. In about 1909 he got to know Franz Marc and two members of the *Neue Künstlervereinigung*, Kandinsky and Jawlensky. In 1911 he helped to edit the *Blaue Reiter* in Munich. In 1912, visiting Paris with Franz Marc, he went to see Delaunay, whose work impressed him enormously. In 1914 he went to Tunisia with Paul Klee, returning with a number of water-colours. He went back to Bonn just before the outbreak of the war in which he was to lose his life. He fell the same year fighting in Champagne.

Though in touch with the painters of the *Blaue Reiter* group, Macke occupies a different position from either Kandinsky or Marc. While they draw their inspiration from their inner worlds, Macke remained attached to his visual experiences. Under the influence of Cubism and above all of Delaunay, form became simplified for him, but he found a more complete interpretation of life in the dynamism of Futurism. Towards the end of his life he did some small abstract works but he never committed himself to abstract art as Marc did. His sensitively drawn figures move in an unreal, iridescent world.

184. Brightly-lit shop windows   1912   p. 127
Oil on canvas, 41³/₈″ × 33¹/₂″
Hanover, State Gallery of Lower Saxony

Alberto Magnelli

Born in Florence in 1888; went to a technical college there. In 1913 he came in contact with Futurism and made friends with its adherents, but he never really belonged to the movement itself. Staying in Paris in 1913 and 1914 he came to know Apollinaire, Picasso, Léger, and Max Jacob. Back in Florence, he produced a series of still-lifes and figure paintings into which he put much of what he had learnt in Paris. His first abstract paintings, done in violent colour, date from 1915. After 1918 he partially returned to representational painting using bold composition and colouring. Since 1931 he has been painting in a geometrical–abstract style, his composition taking the form of balanced configurations constructed according to mathematical rules. He lives in Paris.

185. Confrontation   1952   p. 212
Oil on canvas, 45¹/₄″ × 63³/₄″. Signed and dated at base on right: "Magnelli 52"
Liège, Fernand C. Graindorge

René Magritte

Born at Lessines in 1896; studied at the Académie des Beaux-Arts in Brussels. Travelled widely in France, England, Germany, and Holland. By 1925 his work had already acquired a fantastic character. In 1927 his contacts with the Paris Surrealists led him further along the same road; he adopted Surrealism and has remained faithful to it. He has designed murals for various public buildings in Belgium and has contributed to the Venice Biennales. Lives in Brussels.

Magritte's Surrealism is not derived from the subconscious nor from the world of dreams. It arises from the bizarre aspect he has consciously conferred upon the subject. He gives a thing an unwonted look by putting it in unwonted surroundings. Using all too familiar images, he creates a reality which is perpetually renewed and becomes a source of inexhaustible discovery. With this highly individual conception, Magritte has won a place of his own in the realm of international Surrealism.

186. At the threshold of liberty   1929   p. 190
Oil on canvas, 42⁷/₈″ × 57¹/₂″. Signed at base on left: "Magritte"
Brussels, Urvater collection

Aristide Maillol

Born in 1861 at Banyuls in the Eastern Pyrenees, where he died in 1944. Studied sculpture and painting at the Ecole des Beaux-Arts in Paris. He was then taken on as a pupil by Cabaud, and he did, amongst other things, designs for tapestries.

Influenced by Gauguin and Maurice Denis, he was keenly interested in the revival of handicrafts that grew up along with Symbolism, and he was an assiduous visitor at the Musée Cluny. It was not till 1901, at the age of 40, that he put his hand to sculpture. He then returned to live permanently at Banyuls on the Mediterranean coast. Travelling in Greece in 1906, he was greatly impressed by archaic sculpture. In his own sculpture, he showed from the start a great maturity of style. As opposed to Rodin's dramatic expression and dynamism, Maillol offers us sheer 'presence', calm and static. Working almost entirely on the female figure, Maillol's aim is never portraiture, and he is less complex, more limited, in his work than Rodin. As a sculptor Maillol has close links with archaic as well as with classical Greece.

187. Air (monument to pilots)   1939/43   p. 242
Lead, Ht. 55¹/₈″, Wdth. 100³/₈″
Paris, Dina Vierny Gallery

Casimir Malevitch

Born at Kiev in 1878. Influenced at first by Impressionism and then by Fauvism. Visited Paris in 1912, and on his return became the leader of Cubism in Russia. In 1915 he published the *Suprematist Manifesto* in Moscow. Given a teaching post in Moscow in 1919, he was shifted by the government to Leningrad in 1921. In 1926 he stayed some time in Germany, arranging for the publication of his book *Die gegenstandslose Welt (The World without things)*. He got in touch with Kandinsky and the Bauhaus. Returning to Russia, he died in great privation in 1935.

Suprematism had its roots in both Cubism and Futurism. Malevitch was seeking a radical solution to the problems of form and space with the aid of the simplest geometrical elements such as a black square on a white background, or a circle, triangle and cross. The expression is sacrificed to the construction. His theory of geometrical aesthetics had at one time a certain influence on young Russian painters, and from 1922 onwards had a considerable success in Western Europe in the heyday of the Bauhaus and the *De Stijl* movements. It also left its mark on modern architecture, the applied arts, and industrial design.

188. Suprematist composition (Blue rectangle on purple strip)   1915   p. 17
Oil on canvas, 34⁵/₈″ × 27⁵/₈″
Amsterdam, Stedelijk Museum

189. Suprematist composition (Red Cross on black circle)   1915   p. 209
Oil on canvas, 28¹/₂″ × 20¹/₈″
Amsterdam, Stedelijk Museum

Alfred Manessier

Born at Saint-Ouen, a suburb of Paris, in 1911. Studied at the art-school at Amiens. In 1931 he went to Paris, and studied architecture at the Ecole des Beaux-Arts. He spent a lot of time in the Louvre and attended various art-schools in Montparnasse. At the Académie Ranson he met Bissière. He designed a number of stained glass windows for churches, amongst others at Bresseux in the Jura, Arles, and Basle. He was greatly impressed by the light and the scenery of Holland, where he stayed in 1955. Lives in Paris.

Manessier's point of departure is the visible world. His work is not the expression of an aesthetic theory but an inward experience. After a retreat in the Trappist monastery of Soligny his work took on a religious character. With plastic, purely abstract values, he succeeds in giving a mystic atmosphere to his crucifixions and other biblical subjects. Manessier has thus done something to promote better understanding between the Church and the world of modern and even abstract art.

190. Night 1956   *p. 54*
Oil on canvas, 78³/₄"×59"
Oslo, Ragnar Moltzau collection

Giacomo Manzù

Born at Bergamo in 1908 into a large and poor family. At a very early age he worked in an *atelier de décoration*, and he drew and modelled the heads of his friends. During his military service he managed to study at the Academy of Fine Arts in Verona, his chief preoccupation being the Italian sculpture of the 15th century and, in particular, the work of Donatello. In 1936 he visited Paris, and on his return to Milan he took part in the current controversies among the most advanced artistic groups. In 1941 he received a teaching appointment at the Brera Academy in Milan. He also did bas-reliefs and religious ornaments including *Stations of the Cross* for the church of St. Eugene and a bronze gate for St. Peter's, Rome. In 1948 he won the Prize for sculpture at the Venice Biennale. He lives in Milan.

Manzù has never entirely thrown off the influences that dominated his first period – Rodin, Degas, Medardo Rosso. If he sometimes slips into a certain facile gracefulness he always makes up for it with his remarkable plastic gifts and his great technical accomplishment. A thoroughly *fin de siècle* elegance goes hand in hand with a Latin feeling for powerful form.

191. Dance-step 1955/57   *p. 260*
Bronze, Ht. 78³/₄"
In the artist's possession

Franz Marc

Born in 1880 in Munich, where he received his education. Travelled considerably, visiting Italy, France, Greece, etc. In 1907 he stayed for a while in Paris. In 1910 he went to live at Sindeldorf. Getting to know Kandinsky and Macke, he joined with them in their struggle for a revival of painting. In 1911 he found his true bent and began his famous animal pictures painted in incandescent colours. He became a member of the *Neue Künstlervereinigung* of Munich, and with his friends he published the *Blaue Reiter*, a review that was to inspire the group that adopted that name, and which exhibited for the first time in Munich in 1911 and in Berlin in 1913. On a visit to Paris with Macke in 1912 he went with his friend to see Delaunay, with whom he remained in correspondence. In 1914 he went to live at Ried in Bavaria. Mobilized at the outbreak of war, he was killed at Verdun in 1916.

Starting on naturalistic lines, Marc developed under Kandinsky's influence towards a freer style and the colouring, symbolic in tendency, which is maintained throughout his later work. For him animals symbolized all that was natural and pure, and they formed his favourite subject. Under the influence of Cubism and particularly of Delaunay, he began in 1913 to employ severer and more closely constructed forms, which, richly coloured, melted into a cosmic harmony in which the subject became of minor importance. In his last years Marc plunged whole-heartedly into abstract art based on a lyrical interplay of form.

192. The large blue horses 1911   *p. 27*
Oil on canvas, 40¹/₈"×63"
Minneapolis, Walker Art Center

193. Doe in a flower garden 1913   *p. 126*
Oil on canvas, 21³/₄"×30¹/₂"
Bremen, Art Museum

194. Play of forms 1914   *p. 126*
Oil on canvas, 21¹/₂"×66⁷/₈"
Munich, Otto Stangl Gallery

Louis Marcoussis (Louis Markus)

Born in 1883 in Warsaw, where he studied at the art-school. In 1903, he went to Paris, where he became a friend of La Fresnaye. It was Apollinaire who gave him his pseudonym, Marcoussis, the name of a village near Montlhery. He joined in the experiments of the Cubists, making friends with Braque, Picasso, and Max Jacob. In 1912 he took part in the activities of the *Section d'Or*. Served in the first war. In 1933 he visited the United States. He died at Cusset near Vichy in 1941.

Down to 1907 Marcoussis painted in an Impressionist style. Then, under the influence of Cubism, his work began to be characterised by powerful composition, without, however, neglecting the poetic element, which was preserved in the delicate and subtle colouring. He never ignored the natural order of things, even when introducing symbolic elements. By the vitality of his eternally fresh vision, his landscapes and still-lifes avoid both realistic description and cold stylisation.

195. The table by the balcony 1936   *p. 116*
Oil on canvas, 38¹/₈"×57¹/₂". Signed at base on right:
"Marcoussis"
Paris, National Museum of Modern Art

John Marin

Born in 1870 at Rutherford, New Jersey, he was brought up at Weehawken, N.J., then studied at the art-school and the Art Students' League of Philadelphia. Worked as an architect until the age of 35 when he came to Europe. For five years he lived in Paris, working at private art-schools. Returning to New York, he became associated with Alfred Stieglitz, the most important patron of modern art in America. In 1913 Marin contributed to the Armory Show in New York. Travelled considerably in the United States; he resided alternately at Cliffside, New Jersey, and at Cape Split, Maine. A retrospective exhibition was included in the 1950 Venice Biennale. Died at Cape Split in 1953.

Marin was very active as an etcher, but was still more famous as a water-colour painter. After starting as an Impressionist, he developed an original style based on a very free use of form and colour. With him, the direct expression of the emotion felt takes precedence over problems of form. His work is characterised by intense vitality and great dramatic force.

196. The old salt 1922   p. 135
Water colour, 17″×19³/₄″. Signed and dated at base on right:
"Marin 22"
New York, Metropolitan Museum of Art
(Alfred Stieglitz collection)

197. Movement No. 2 (The black sun) 1926   p. 135
Water colour. 21⁵/₈″×26³/₈″. Signed and dated at base on
right: "Marin 26"
New York, Metropolitan Museum of Art
(Alfred Stieglitz collection)

Marino Marini

Born in 1901 at Pistoia in Tuscany. His artistic education was begun at the Academy of Fine Arts in Florence and continued in Paris in 1928 and 1929, after which he settled in Milan. He taught sculpture at a neighbouring town, Monza, until 1940, when he transferred to the Brera in Milan. Has travelled considerably in Europe and paid several visits to the United States. He has a second studio at Forte dei Marmi near Pisa where he often works.

At every exhibition of modern sculpture one is struck by the importance of Marini and his great influence on his period. Archaic culture has interested the leading sculptors since the beginning of this century, but he was the first really to assimilate it, which he did in a very individual style. His work is a meeting ground of tradition and modern expression. With an extraordinary élan he expresses his forebodings and his dreams in vigorous and violent form which is, however always kept in hand. Marini is also a distinguished print-maker and painter. His great feeling for colour is, in his sculpture, expressed in the patina. He does horses and riders, dancers, nudes, and portrait busts. The last are as convincing by their likeness as by their sculptural quality.

198. Juggler 1940   p. 262
Bronze. Ht. 38¹/₈″
In the artist's possession

199. Horse and rider 1953/54   p. 70
Painted wood, Ht. 83⁷/₈″, Base 80³/₄″×47⁵/₈″
In the artist's possession

Albert Marquet

Born in 1875 at Bordeaux, which he left in 1890 to go to Paris, where he attended the Ecole des Arts Décoratifs and the Ecole des Beaux-Arts. In 1897 he was working in Gustave Moreau's studio, where he met Matisse. The two made friends and became brothers-in-arms. He did some copying at the Louvre (Poussin, Claude Lorraine, Chardin) but was chiefly influenced by Van Gogh, the Impressionists, and Japanese art. In 1898, accompanied by Matisse, he painted his first landscapes. As soon as Fauvism started he joined the movement, and he exhibited at the Salon des Indépendants and at the Salon d'Automne. From 1910 to 1912 he spent much of his time travelling. Fascinated by the activity of ports, he visited Le Havre, Naples, Hamburg, Rotterdam, Tangier, etc. After 1925 he did most of his work in water-colour. He died in Paris in 1947.

Although one of the first champions of Fauvism, Marquet is a somewhat isolated figure. He did not retain the Fauvist principles of his first period, and in the end adopted a decidedly impressionistic style. Though in his early days he did some excellent portraits and figure paintings, he is now remembered chiefly for his paintings of ports, and of Paris – the Cité, the bridges, the quays. He portrays nature, not as a bold transposition in artistic terms, but as a simple poetic vision.

200. Portrait of André Rouveyre 1904   p. 104
Oil on canvas, 36¹/₄″×24″. Signed and dated at base on left:
"Marquet 1904"
Paris, National Museum of Modern Art

Arturo Martini

Born in 1889 at Treviso, into a poor family. He learnt craftsmanship from a goldsmith and then a potter, receiving at the same time the beginnings of an artistic education, which was continued when he became the pupil of the sculptor Carlini. Went to Venice and then to Paris, where he arrived in 1907 at the same time as Medardo Rosso. Two years later he took lessons from Hildebrand in Munich. In 1920 he joined the Valori Plastici group in Rome. He remained passionately fond of ceramics and produced important works in this medium. Executed numerous statues and reliefs for the decoration of buildings, some of which may be seen in Milan. In 1945 he published his book, Scultura, Lingua Morta. He died in Milan in 1947.

Martini's sculptures are done in a tortured modern spirit, which seeks to go beyond the great traditions of the past by introducing living problems into sculpture and giving free rein to a powerful imagination. Open to outside influences – German classicism, Maillol, Futurism – he has produced work of great diversity. As a supporter of a more absolute style, he was violently critical of the older revolutionaries, such as Boccioni. His work is very unequal, but excellent at his best moments. He is a leading figure in many of the experimental movements which succeeded Italian Futurism.

201. Thirst 1934   p. 262
Stone, Ht. 30³/₄″, Wdth. 43¹/₄″
Milan, Civic Gallery of Modern Art

Marcello Mascherini

Born in 1916 at Udine. When he was four his parents moved to Trieste, where later he entered the Istituto Industriale. He contributed to the artistic life of Trieste, not only as a sculptor, but also as a designer of scenery and costumes for theatre and ballet. He undertook decorative work for Italian liners and for the Milan Triennale. He works in wood, stone, and bronze, and also does lithographs and drawings.

Mascherini was stimulated by Martini's work, and also by Etruscan civilisation and the art of the Italian Renaissance. Modern woman figures largely in his sculpture, which is characterized by a keen sense of line and form and by an elegant, somewhat mannered, distortion. He stands out from other Italian sculptors by the original stylisation of his nudes, which are made to seem both mystical and real.

202. La Franca 1952   p. 261
Bronze, Ht. 70⁷/₈″
Otterlo, Kröller-Müller Rijksmuseum

André Masson

Born in 1896 at Balagny, Oise. In 1912, after studying at the Brussels Academy, he went to Paris on the advice of Emile Verhaeren. He made friends with Juan Gris and came under the influence of Cubism. In 1923 he produced his first symbolic picture. From 1925 he was for a while associated with the Surrealists, contributing to their exhibitions, but he was not included in 1928. From 1934 to 1936 he was working in Catalonia. During the last war he was in America. In 1947 he settled in Aix-en-Provence, where he is still living.

Masson deals with all the violent emotions and actions of mankind and animals and expresses an aggressive, convulsive eroticism. He transcended his early Cubist style by means of symbols suggested to him by a world full of drama and despair. Living in the south of France seems to have brought some serenity into his work, which till then verged on the chaotic.

203. The oncoming of night 1956   *p. 235*
Oil on canvas, 39³/₈″ × 74³/₄″. Signed at base on right: "A. Masson"
Paris, Louise Leiris Gallery

Henri Matisse

Born in 1869 at Le Cateau near Cambrai. At first he studied law, then turned to painting in 1890, beginning at the Académie Julian, then becoming the pupil of Gustave Moreau. In 1898 he travelled in Corsica. The following year he went back to Paris, where he came under the influence of Cézanne. He was one of the founders of the *Salon d'Automne* in 1903. Working at Saint-Tropez he came in contact with Signac and was influenced by Neo-impressionism. In 1905 he took part in the first exhibition of the Fauves. Travelled in Germany, Spain, and Russia, and lived in Morocco from 1911 to 1913. Worked for Diaghilev. In 1930 he visited the United States and Tahiti. In 1938 he went to live in Cimiez, a suburb of Nice, but in 1943 moved to Vence, where from 1949 to 1951 he worked on the chapel. In 1950 he was awarded the *Grand Prix* for painting at the Venice Biennale. He died in Nice in 1954.

After going through a Neo-impressionist phase, Matisse came under the influence of Cézanne and also became interested in Divisionism. Fortified by these influences, his own personality began to assert itself. He became the undisputed master of Fauvism, with his simplified forms, and bright, ungradated colours. Matisse may be regarded as the apostle of 'pure' painting, in that he aims only at visual, sensual pleasure. His pictorial genius, his elegant taste, and his very French feeling for balance are plainly visible in the harmony of his happy colouring and the graceful arabesques of his still-lifes, nudes, and interiors. The Vence Chapel, of which he was both architect and decorator, may be regarded as the summit of his work. The painting of Matisse, modern as it is, yet at the same time rooted in French tradition, forms a bridge between the past and the present, and constitutes one of the major contributions to contemporary art.

204. The red carpet 1906   *p. 10*
Canvas, 39³/₈″ × 55¹/₈″. Signed at base on right: "Henri Matisse"
Grenoble, Museum of Grenoble (Agutte-Sembat collection)

205. Capuchines dancing c. 1910   *p. 109*
Signed at base on right: "Matisse"
Moscow, Pushkin Museum

206. Still-life with goldfish 1911   *p. 106*
Oil on canvas, 57⁷/₈″ × 38⁵/₈″
Moscow, Pushkin Museum

207. The Studio (The painter's studio) 1911   *p. 108*
Oil on canvas, 67³/₄″ × 80³/₄″. Signed and dated at base on right: "Henri Matisse 1911"
Moscow, Pushkin Museum

208. Still-life with Spanish shawls 1910   *p. 110*
Oil on canvas, 35″ × 45⁵/₈″. Signed at base on right: "Henri Matisse"
Leningrad, The Hermitage

209. Portrait of Madame Matisse 1913   *p. 105*
Oil on canvas, 57⁷/₈″ × 38⁵/₈″. Signed at base on right: "Henri Matisse"
Leningrad, The Hermitage

210. The painter and his model 1917   *p. 107*
Oils, 57⁷/₈″ × 38⁸/₈″
Paris, National Museum of Modern Art

Roberto Sebastiano Matta Echaurren

Born in 1912 in Santiago, Chile. In 1934 he began studying architecture under Le Corbusier. From 1938 to 1947 he belonged to the Surrealist movement. In 1939 he went to live in the United States, where he made friends with Marcel Duchamp. Went to Mexico in 1941, then worked successively in Madrid, Paris, and New York. Lived in Rome from 1950 to 1953. Now lives in Paris.

Passionately interested in psychology and psychiatry, like all Surrealists, Matta Echaurren is a student of Freud. On the other hand he is also interested in physics, mathematics, and architecture. Dreams and mental states are the sources of inspiration of his fantastic creations, in which, under the influence of Duchamp, he often introduces rigorous construction. At other times he bursts into a blaze of colour as though heralding the nuclear age.

211. Giving light without pain 1955   *p. 236*
Oil on canvas, 76³/₄″ × 118¹/₈″. Signed on back: "Matta"
Brussels, Urvater collection

George Minne

Born at Ghent in 1866. Studied architecture at the school of fine arts there, at the same time taking lessons in sculpture and painting. First became known in 1889 as a member of *Les XX*. Staying in Paris, he made the acquaintance of Rodin. He became associated with the Symbolists. In 1895 he began working in Brussels, but in 1899 he settled at Laethem-Saint-Martin. A colony of Flemish artists, the first Laethem group, formed round him. He was in England during the first war, was given a title in 1930, and died at Laethem in 1941.

George Minne was a sculptor, draughtsman and printmaker. His impressionistic beginnings were greatly influenced by Rodin. Later he was attracted by Gothic art and by Claus Sluter. Slowly he developed a sober stylisation of the human figure which he endeavoured to make both spiritual and static. His most important work was done at the end of the last century. His world-famous fountain with the kneeling ephebes is regarded as his *chef-d'œuvre*. A mystic sentiment underlies his work, which is both Symbolist and Realist, and which did much to foster the revival of Belgian sculpture.

212. The relics-bearer 1897   *p. 244*
Quenast stone, Ht. 27⁵/₈″, Wdth. 10⁵/₈″, Dpth. 6³/₄″
Brussels, Marcel Cuvelier collection

Mirko (Mirko Basaldella)

Born at Udine in 1910. His early years were spent in Venice, Florence, and Monza, near Milan, at the last of which he attended the art-school. In 1932 he became the pupil of Arturo Martini in Milan. In 1936 he spent some time in Paris, with his brother, the painter Afro. But his work remained representational under Martini's influence. It was only in 1947, after experimenting with Cubism, that he turned to abstract art. He works in the most diverse materials in a personal style that remains eternally fresh. Technically he improved on older methods and invented new ones. His subjects are very varied, ranging from exotic idols to industrial design.

213. Stump motif 1957   p. 283
Black cement, Ht. 47^1/$_4$"
In the artist's possession

Joan Miró

Born in 1893 at Montroig near Barcelona. He studied at Barcelona, then, in 1915, started working on his own. In 1919 he went to Paris, and thenceforward divided his time between Barcelona and Paris. He kept in touch with the Picasso circle as well as with the Surrealists. Spain was closed to him by the civil war, but he was able to go back in 1946. Between 1944 and 1946 he did a lot of work in ceramics in collaboration with L. Artigas. He has also done some sculpture and has been very active in engraving and lithography.

Miró's work cannot be classed among that of either the Cubists or the Surrealists. Still less can it be considered abstract. Like Klee and Kandinsky, by whom he was influenced, he developed his painting along the margins of reality, using objects in recognizable fragments or indicated by signs or symbols. Colour, line, and composition stem from his inward life and poetic imagination. A great breath of lyricism emanates from his work which transports us into a clear, limpid world.

Miró's influence, which extends even into the realm of experimental painting, is due to the purity of his intuition and the subtlety of his texture. In Miró poetry and painting blend.

214. Tilled earth 1923/24   p. 185
Oil on canvas, 26"×36^5/$_8$"
Philadelphia, Mr. & Mrs. Henry Clifford collection

215. Carnival of Harlequin 1924/25   p. 43
Oil on canvas, 26"×37^3/$_8$"
Buffalo, Allbright Art Gallery

216. The grasshopper 1926   p. 187
Oil on canvas, 57^1/$_2$"×44^7/$_8$". Date and signature, "1926 Joan Miró", form part of the composition in the lower portion of the picture
Brussels, Pierre Janlet collection

217. People and rhythm 1934   p. 186
Oil on canvas, 37^3/$_8$"×148^3/$_8$"
Brussels, Philippe Dotremont collection

218. Composition 1953   p. 187
Oil on canvas, 72^3/$_8$"×64^1/$_8$"
Paris, Maeght Gallery

Paula Modersohn-Becker

Born in Dresden in 1876, but was brought up in Bremen. Received her first drawing lessons in London, where she stayed in 1892. She then went to study at an art-school in

Berlin. In 1900 she visited Paris for the first time. In 1901 she married the painter Otto Modersohn. Lived at Worpswede and became friendly with Rainer Maria Rilke. Stayed many times in Paris. On her last visit, in 1906, she was greatly struck by the work of Cézanne and Gauguin. Died at Worpswede in 1907 at the age of 31.

Her point of departure was the Naturalist school of Worpswede. Under the impetus of a great love of nature, she discovered new spiritual and expressive outlets in painting which were to give rise later to German Expressionism. For, with her sombre and melancholy style, she was, in her short career, the real founder of that movement.

219. Portrait of Rainer Maria Rilke 1906   p. 123
Oil on canvas, 13^3/$_8$"×10^1/$_4$". Initialled at base on left: "P.M.B."
Bremen, Ludwig Roselius collection

Amedeo Modigliani

Born at Leghorn in 1884, a descendant, on his mother's side, of Spinoza. His father was a banker. Modigliani's youth was an unhappy one. He had to stop all work for a time on account of his health. He learnt the elements of painting from a landscape painter of Leghorn. In 1906 he went to Paris where he lived a bohemian life. Cézanne's work came as a revelation to him and exercized a decisive influence, though he was also influenced by Toulouse-Lautrec and Picasso. In his early works he was already practising some distortion in order to enhance the expression. Encouraged by Brancusi he began to do some sculpture, and in this one can detect the influence of Negro art. From 1917 and the following years came a series of nudes and portraits of working-class people. In 1918 his work began to be known, but, with his health undermined by illness and privation, he died in Paris in 1920. His wife Jeanne Hébuterne, who had borne him a daughter, killed herself on the day of his funeral.

Modigliani had known all the afflictions of the *peintre maudit*. Like many another foreigner, he was a genuine member of the Ecole de Paris, though he never threw off the traces of his Italian origin. Faithful to the Tuscan tradition, his work remained linear. Though striving for great elegance in colour, he expresses himself primarily in the linear quality of his paintings. All his figures are precisely though delicately outlined by expressive curves.

Modigliani is one of the most outstanding figures of modern Italian art. He had no predecessors; he had no successors.

220. Caryatid 1912   p. 246
Stone, Ht. 28^3/$_4$"
Brussels, Baron Boël collection

221. Italian woman   p. 154
Oil on canvas, 40^1/$_4$"×26^3/$_8$". Signed top right: "Modigliani"
New York, Metropolitan Museum of Art (The Chester Dale collection)

222. Red-haired woman with pendant 1917   p. 29
Oil on canvas, 36^5/$_8$"×23^5/$_8$". Signed top right: "Modigliani"
Brussels, Henri Belien collection

Làzlo Moholy-Nagy

Born in 1895 at Bacsbarsod in Hungary. Studied law in Budapest. Wounded during the first war, he began to paint during his convalescence. He became interested in

the advanced school of Russian painters, such as Kandinsky and Lissitzky. By 1920 his work had become thoroughly abstract. He was given a post at the Dessau Bauhaus, and he edited the *Bauhausbücher*. He himself wrote several books on experiments with the new art techniques. In 1922 his *Buch Neuer Künstler*, an anthology of the work of *avant-garde* artists, was published in Vienna. In 1928 he left the Bauhaus and began travelling in Europe. In 1934 he visited Amsterdam, a year later London. There he produced the first of those works combining painting and sculpture which he called 'space modulators'. In 1937 he went to live in Chicago where he founded the New Bauhaus and later his own private art-school, the School of Design. His work, *The New Vision*, was published in New York in 1946. He died the same year in Chicago.
Moholy-Nagy was an out-and-out experimentalist, and he worked in many fields – painting, photography, graphic arts, art-theory and art-education. He was the most versatile of the Constructivists. His didactic works are an inexhaustible mine of ideas, examples, and original solutions to the problems of modern art. His various researches, and particularly his experiments in space and form and his exploration of new materials such as plexiglas, galalith, copper, aluminium, etc., have had an unquestionable influence on the style of modern life.

223. Ch Beata 1. 1939   *p. 211*
Oil on canvas, 46¹⁄₈″ × 46⁷⁄₈″
New York, The Solomon R. Guggenheim Museum

Piet Mondrian

Born in 1872 at Amersfoort in Holland. His father, a schoolmaster, was against his taking up an artistic career, but Mondrian finally had his way, and went in 1892 to study art in Amsterdam. At this time he began to paint a number of landscapes. Going to Paris in 1914 he came under the influence of the Cubists. When the war started he went back to Holland, but returned to Paris in 1918. In 1920 he published his essay on Neo-Plasticism. In 1938, with the threat of another war, he took refuge in England. When the air-raids started in 1940 he moved on to New York, where the great significance of his work was soon recognized. He died in 1944.
Starting with Naturalism and passing through Pointillism and Cubism, Mondrian's painting turned towards the rigorous laws of abstraction, arriving eventually at a system of strong verticals and horizontals and pure primary colours. For twenty years Mondrian had been groping for his own style, which he himself called Neo-Plasticism. In 1917, with Van Doesburg and a few others, he founded the review entitled *De Stijl*, which was the mouthpiece of a movement that was destined to play an eminent part in the evolution of modern art and architecture. Having formulated the fundamental principles of this movement, Mondrian remained faithful to them for the rest of his life.

224. Oval composition (trees) 1913   *p. 207*
Oil on canvas, 37″ × 30³⁄₄″. Signed at base on right:
"Mondrian"
Amsterdam, Stedelijk Museum

225. Composition with red, yellow and blue 1921   *p. 208*
Oil on canvas, 31¹⁄₂″ × 19⁵⁄₈″. Signed and dated at base on
left: "P.M. 21"
The Hague, Gemeente Museum

226. Victory boogie-woogie 1943/44 (unfinished)   *p. 14*
Oil and scraps of paper stuck on canvas (diamond-shaped),
50″ × 50″
New York, Museum of Modern Art

Claude Monet

Born in Paris in 1840. Spent his youth in Le Havre where he knew Boudin, who interested him in open-air painting. In 1857 he joined the Académie Suisse in Paris where he met Pissarro. In 1862 at Gleyre's studio he met and became friendly with Renoir, Sisley and Bazille; they worked together in the forest of Fontainebleau. At the beginning his work was influenced by Courbet. Visiting London with Pissarro in 1871, he became an admirer of Turner. From 1874 he worked in Argenteuil with Renoir and Manet and took part in most of the Impressionists' exhibitions. He also painted the famous 'series', of which the *Cathedral of Rouen*, *Windmills*, and *Water-lilies* are still the most complete expression of his art.

227. White water-lilies 1919   *p. 74*
Oil on canvas, 39¹⁄₄″ × 78³⁄₄″
Paris, Pierre Durand-Ruel collection

Henry Moore

Born in 1898 at Castleford in Yorkshire, into a miner's family. He was intended to be a schoolmaster. Injured by poison gas during the first war. In 1919, with a scholarship, he began studying art at Leeds, and continued his training at the Royal College of Art. Visits to France and Italy (1921) completed his art education. On his return he was offered a post at the Royal College, and later began teaching at the Chelsea Art School. Has executed many official commissions. During the last war he produced his famous series of drawings of air-raid shelters. Moore has travelled frequently in Europe, particularly in France, Spain, and Italy. In 1945 he was given an honorary degree by the University of Leeds. In 1948 he won the Grand Prix for sculpture at the Venice Biennale. Lives at Much Hadham, Herts.
Influenced by Brancusi and archaic sculpture, Moore developed a style that sometimes comes near to pure abstraction, but, for the most part, his work is essentially representational. Despite its human and tragic content, it gives an impression of calm grandeur. Moore is regarded as one of the conciliators between the representational and abstract camps, and he exerts a considerable influence on numerous young sculptors today.

228. Recumbent figure 1950/51   *p. 280*
Bronze, Ht. 41³⁄₄″, Wdth. 88⁵⁄₈″, Dpth. 29¹⁄₂″
Paris, National Museum of Modern Art

229. Glenkiln Cross 1956   *p. 279*
Bronze, 132¹⁄₄″
In the artist's possession

Giorgio Morandi

Born in 1890 at Bologna, where he studied at the Academy of Fine Arts. He has travelled little and is one of the handful of Italian artists who have never been to Paris. His first pictures date from 1911. A year later he started etching and engraving. At first he was influenced by Cézanne, though he knew his work only in reproductions. In 1914 he became a member of the Rome *Secessione*. From 1916 onwards he was painting his celebrated series of still-lifes. After a short Futurist phase he was for a while (1918–1920) associated with the *Pittura Metafisica*. Next he was associated with the *Valori Plastici* movement. But he developed his own style independently, a style that was at once simple and sober. In 1957 he was awarded the Prize of the São Paulo Biennale. He lives in Bologna.

Morandi took the metaphysical school of Italian painting to its logical conclusion, far from Ferrara and the influence of Chirico and Carrà. His drawings are works of linear magic, in which his great intelligence and sensibility reinforce his imagination. His universe is limited to the quiet, intimate world of the still-life, itself restricted to a few simple, shadowy objects in sober colours. And he uses delicate tones even in his paintings, which often come near to *grisaille*. The quality of his colouring has had a great influence on such painters as Scipione, Mafai, Cagli.

230. *Metaphysical still-life   1918*   *p. 144*
Oil on canvas, 21¹/₄″ × 25¹/₄″
Milan, private collection

231. *Still-life   1957*   *p. 144*
Oil on canvas
Milan, private collection

Richard Mortensen

Born in 1910 in Copenhagen, where he studied for two years at the Academy, after which he worked on his own. On a visit to Berlin he came across Kandinsky's work. It was then that he decided to devote himself entirely to painting. In 1933 he produced his first abstract works. In 1937 he went to live in Paris. Later he went back to Copenhagen to organize an exhibition of the abstract works of the Parisian school; but in 1947 he returned to Paris, where he still lives. He and his fellow-countryman Jacobsen, the sculptor, belong to the group which is centred round the Denise René Gallery.

Mortensen's huge abstract pictures are composed of geometrical surfaces, and simple lines painted in vivid colours. His work, distinguished, harmonious, and elegant, is not the result of any facile skill but of a great spiritual discipline and the determination to arrive at a simple and precise plastic composition.

232. *Houlgate   1955*   *p. 224*
Oil on canvas, 63³/₄″ × 51¹/₈″
Paris, Denise René Gallery

Véra Ignatevna Mouchina

Born at Riga in 1889. Studied in private art-schools in Moscow and then in the Ecole des Beaux-Arts, Paris. She contributed to important exhibitions in the Soviet Union and abroad (India, Indonesia, Finland). Her sculpture was also shown at the Paris Exposition Universelle, the New York World Fair, and the 16th, 19th, and 28th Venice Biennale. Died in Moscow in 1953.

233. *The partisan   1942*   *p. 264*
Bronze, Ht. 18¹/₈″, Wdth. 10⁵/₈″, Dpth. 9¹/₂″
Moscow, Tretiakov Museum

Otto Mueller

Born in 1874 at Liebau in German Silesia. Learnt lithography at Breslau, then went as an art-student to Dresden. In 1908 he went to live in Berlin where he came in contact with Erich Heckel and in 1910 joined *Die Brücke*. For a time he lived with Kirchner near Prague. Served in the German army during the first war. In 1919 he was appointed to a teaching post in Breslau, where he died in 1930.

Müller was the last to join the group of artists who formed *Die Brücke*. His decorative compositions, painted without depth, are characterised by firm expressive outlines and big splashes of colour. Gauguin's influence on German art is particularly noticeable in him. Müller was well known for his paintings of gypsies, whom he used to express his attitude to society, just as Kirchner did in his street-scenes or Heckel in his studies of poor people. Müller's paintings and lithographs have the same romantic-lyrical tendency that is found in Heckel.

234. *Gypsies with sunflower   1927*   *p. 162*
Oil on canvas, 57¹/₈″ × 41³/₈″
Sarrebruck, Saarland Museum

Edvard Munch

Born at Löten in Norway in 1863. When his studies in Oslo came to an end in 1890, he left the country, living abroad for the next 18 years, chiefly in Paris, the South of France, Italy, and Germany. Impressed by Van Gogh, Seurat, and Toulouse-Lautrec, he added more colour to his palette. In 1908, after a period of disillusionment he returned to settle in his own country, where he worked in retirement on one of his estates. Between 1909 and 1911 he painted frescos for Oslo University, and in 1921–1922 he did some for a factory there, in a freer style, both as regards colour and composition. During his last years he painted a series of extremely able self-portraits. He died in 1944 on his Ekely estate near Oslo.

With Munch the problem of form always takes second place to the emotional mood, reflecting, no doubt, at any rate during the first half of his career, his lonely and melancholy life. He combines the unreality of the dream with an urgent and threatening reality. His spiritual world is haunted by life and death, woman and love. In 1890 he began working on a series of paintings, *The Frieze of Life*, of which the one here included, *The Dance of Life*, is the central part. The same themes are found again in his drawings, which are sometimes even more expressive than his paintings.

His influence was felt chiefly in Germany, where *Die Brücke* was formed under his influence. Munch may be considered to rank with Van Gogh and Ensor as one of the precursors of Expressionism.

235. *The dance of life   1899/1900*   *p. 85*
Canvas, 49¹/₄″ × 74³/₄″. *Signed at base on left: "E. Munch"*
Oslo, National Gallery

Paul Nash

Born in London in 1889. On leaving St. Paul's School he went to the Slade. During the first war he was wounded at Ypres. In 1917 he was appointed as one of the official artists to the War Office. He painted many large pictures for official bodies, such as the Imperial War Museum and the Canadian War Records. In 1933 he was one of the founders of *Unit One*, a group of modern painters, architects, and sculptors. Was president of the Society of Industrial Artists. In 1938 he contributed to the Venice Biennale. Besides his oil paintings, he did water-colours, and designs for textiles, scenery, costumes, and ceramics. Died at Boscombe in 1946.

Nash's work blends two contradictory tendencies. On the one hand was a keen interest in all the currents of modern art between the two wars, particularly Surrealism; on the other was a profound attachment to nature and to landscape. Both are reflected in his work. The wealth of his imagination recalls William Blake. Whatever subject he touched, his treatment of it was stamped with a lyricism which links him with the best tradition of British water-colourists.

236. The eclipse of the sunflower 1945 *p. 180*
Oils, 26³|₄″×35⁷|₈″. Signed at base on left: "Nash"
London, The British Council

Ernst Wilhelm Nay

Born in 1902 in Berlin, and studied at the art-school there, being for some years a pupil of Karl Hofer. He was also influenced by Kirchner. After Expressionist beginnings and a phase of Neo-Realism, he turned in 1948 towards abstract art. Belonged to the German group *Zen*, which gave an exhibition in Munich in 1955. Lives in Cologne. In his work, Nay reconciles the formal demands of non-representational art with the violently contrasted colours of Expressionism. The subject is reduced to a mere allusion or a point of departure, space is superficialized, and the rhythmical, dynamic, sometimes explosive colour creates another world, which is the expression of a cosmic feeling.

237. Alpha 1957 *p. 216*
Oil on canvas, 45⁵|₈″×35″. Signed and dated at base on right: "Nay 57"
In the artist's possession

Ben Nicholson

Born in 1894 at Denham, Bucks. Studied at the Slade. Travelled often to the Continent, staying frequently in Paris, where he made contact with the Cubists. In 1933 he joined the *Abstraction-Création* group. In 1934 he produced his first geometrical bas-reliefs. The same year he met Mondrian, who later became his neighbour in Hampstead (1938–1940). In 1951 he painted some enormous murals for the Festival of Britain. Won the Carnegie Prize in 1952 and the Guggenheim Prize in 1956. Lived at St. Ives till 1958, but is now living at Ascona.
After coming temporarily under various influences from the Continent, Nicholson developed his own personal style. His work hovers between a rigid purism, abstraction, and representation. He developed Mondrian's theories in a series of severely formal bas-reliefs, but he refuses to adhere to any dogma, and he also paints various kinds of still-lifes and landscapes. His composition is characterised by pale, subtle colouring, and by a rhythmic subdivision of the surface. With its classic harmony, his translucent and lyrical painting has exercised a great influence on the British artists of today. Nicholson's work is England's chief contribution to non-representational art.

238. White Relief (1st version) 1938 *p. 211*
Oil on composition board, 44¹|₂″×69¹|₄″
In the artist's possession

239. Crete 1956 *p. 50*
Oil, 79⁷|₈″×100″
Dr. Felicitas Vogler Nicholson collection

Sidney Nolan

Born in Melbourne in 1917 and studied at the National Art Gallery School. In 1950 he was enabled to stay in Italy by a grant from the Italian government. Worked for a time in Greece. Nolan's painting is a reaction against the academic training he had received. In his early work he liked to depict the stories that had grown up round the Australian highwayman, Ned Kelly. Later, after an expedition to Central Australia, he produced a series of pictures dealing with animal carcasses (see the one reproduced here). During his stay in Italy he did a series of Crucifixions. All his pictures are stamped with his taste for the fantastic and his leaning towards Surrealism. Nolan presents us with an original aspect of present-day Australian art. He is now living in London.

240. Ram after the flood 1955 *p. 238*
Oil on masonite, 41³|₈″×35³|₈″. Initialled and dated on left towards the base: "N. 55"
London, Mrs. Cynthia Nolan collection

Emil Nolde (Emil Hansen)

Born in 1867 at Nolde in German Schleswig; studied at the Kunstgewerbeschule in Flensburg and later at Karlsruhe. In 1892 he began teaching at the Fachschule at Saint-Gall. Lived alternately in Munich, Paris, and Copenhagen. In 1904 he adopted the name of his native village as a pseudonym. In 1906 he went to live in Berlin and joined *Die Brücke*. His first religious pictures were painted in 1909. In 1911, on a visit to Holland and Belgium, he met James Ensor. In 1912 he became associated with the painters of the *Blaue Reiter*. Spent a considerable time travelling in the Far East and the Pacific. After the first war he divided his time between Berlin and his country house at Seebüll in Schleswig. In 1933 his work was condemned as degenerate by the Nazis and in 1941 he was forbidden to paint at all. He died at Seebüll in 1956.
Nolde worked both in oil and water-colour, as well as doing a large number of drawings. His work is dominated by feeling, much more than by intellect, and by an extraordinary sense of colour. His violent and direct style goes straight to the heart of the matter, with an expressive, sometimes brutally expressive, power. As a result of his close communion with nature, he is in his own way a visionary and a mystic. He gives a religious feeling to the most primitive sensuality, and his Expressionism fostered the revival of religious art in Germany.

241. The legend of Maria Aegyptiaca 1912 *p. 128*
Oil on canvas, centre panel: The conversion, 41³|₈″×47¹|₄″. Signed at base on right: "Emil Nolde"
Left wing: At the port of Alexandria, 33⁷|₈″×39³|₈″. Signed at base on left: "Emil Nolde"
Right wing: Death in the desert, 33⁷|₈″×39³|₈″. Signed centre base: "Emil Nolde"
Hamburg, Art Museum

242. The lemon orchard 1933 *p. 162*
Oil on canvas, 28³|₄″×35″. Signed at base on right: "Emil Nolde"
Bad Homburg, Dr. Max Lütze collection

Isidore Opsomer

Born in 1879 at Lierre in Belgium. Began his studies there, continuing them at the Académie Royale and the Institut Supérieur des Beaux-Arts at Antwerp. Travelled in Europe, visiting Italy, France, Germany, Austria. In 1905 he took up an appointment at the Académie Royale, Antwerp. In 1914 the war drove him to England. Later he moved to Holland, where he made the acquaintance of Breitner and Sluyters. In 1919 he became a teacher at the

Institut Supérieur National des Beaux-Arts of which he became the Director seven years later. In 1922 he began a long series of portraits. In 1935 he became Director of the Académie Royale, Antwerp, and in 1940 he received a title. He lives in Antwerp.

After a slow development, Opsomer outgrew the style which had characterised his early work, and in this he was greatly helped by his stay in Holland during the first war. Stimulated by the later Impressionism of Breitner, he developed an individual style in his landscapes and still-lifes, which have something really great about them. He later became his country's leading portrait painter, producing works in which a direct vision of great vitality goes hand in hand with a remarkable feeling for space.

243. Professor J. Muls   1942   *p. 200*
Oil on canvas, $31^1/_8'' \times 25^5/_8''$. Signed, top left: "Opsomer"
Brussels, Royal Belgian Museum of Fine Art

José Clemente Orozco

Born at Ciudad Cuzman in Mexico in 1883. Began by studying agriculture, then switched to art in 1908. When the revolution broke out in 1913, he became a caricaturist. Made friends with his fellow-countrymen Rivera and Siqueiros. From 1923 he was at work with others on the huge frescos being painted in Mexico City. Lived in the United States for four years from 1930, and spent some time in Europe. He wrote his autobiography. Died in Mexico City in 1949.

Less influenced than Rivera by European movements, Orozco's work was inspired by the folklore and art of the Aztecs. Working in a realistic, monumental style, he placed his art at the service of politics, the claim of the common man for a place in the world being the substance of his message. Orozco was one of the pioneers of modern art in Mexico, and the interest of the English and the Americans in the new Mexican school is largely due to him.

244. Fighting   1920   *p. 198*
Oil on canvas, $26^1/_4'' \times 34^5/_8''$. Signed at base on left: "Orozco"
Mexico, Dr. Alvar Carrillo Gil collection

Constant Permeke

Born at Antwerp in 1886. Studied at the Academies of Bruges and Ghent. Went in 1906 to live at Laethem-Saint-Martin, and became the leader of the second Laethem group, which he formed with Frits Van den Berghe, the brothers Gustave and Léon de Smet and various other artists and writers. Lived for a while at Ostend. Mobilized in 1914, he was seriously wounded, evacuated to England, and invalided out of the army. His first Expressionist works belong to this period. After the war, he returned to Belgium and settled at Jabbeke, where there is now a Permeke Museum. In 1936 he took up sculpture. In 1951 he worked for a time in Britanny. He died at Ostend in 1952.

Painter, draughtsman, and sculptor, Permeke is the outstanding exponent of Flemish Expressionism. His inspiration was derived from the country, the sea, and the lives of the peasants and other simple people around him. A child of nature, rooted in the soil, Permeke expressed himself spontaneously, and in his Expressionist style he reflected the primitive feelings of man in vigorous and sombre colours and simple monumental forms.

245. Peasant family with cat   1928   *p. 34*
Oil on canvas, $65^3/_8'' \times 71^5/_8''$. Signed and dated at base on left: "28 Permeke"
Brussels, Gustave von Geluwe collection

246. The sow   1929   *p. 170*
Oil on canvas, $88^5/_8'' \times 78^3/_4''$. Signed at base on left: "Permeke"
Waalre, Tims van Bakel collection

247. Dawn   1935   *p. 170*
Oil on canvas, $74^3/_4'' \times 79^7/_8''$. Signed at base on left: "Permeke"
Reux, Baron Alix de Rothschild collection

Antoine Pevsner

Born at Orel in 1886. After studying art in Kiev and St. Petersburg, he went to Paris in 1913 and formed a greater attachment to it than did his brother Gabo. Pevsner did not stay long on this occasion, however, since he spent the war years in Norway. Enthusiastic about the Russian revolution in 1917 he soon returned to his country, where he was asked to undertake the reform of art education. Made friends with Malevich. In 1923, disheartened by what was going on in Russia, he returned via Germany to Paris, where he is still working, and where he is accepted as a member of the Ecole de Paris. Since 1946 he has belonged to the *Salon des Réalités Nouvelles*.

In collaboration with his brother, Gabo, Pevsner developed the theory of Constructivism which, according to the 1920 Manifesto, was to liberate sculpture from academism and subjectivism both in regard to materials and forms. After undergoing the influence of Cubism, his sculpture became purified in character: he succeeded in reviving the Futurist idea of the simultaneity of time and space. Pevsner often uses wire and metal rods, giving curved surfaces an aerodynamic quality. His sculpture is essentially movement crystallized in space.

248. Dynamic projection at 30°   1950/51   *p. 68*
Bronze, $39^3/_8'' \times 98^3/_8''$
Paris, National Museum of Modern Art

Francis Picabia

Born in 1879 in Paris, his mother being French, his father Cuban. He began painting at the age of 16, working in Cormon's studio. From the first, he was successful. He belonged variously to the Cubist, Dadaist and Surrealist movements. In 1912–1913 he was in the United States, and he took part in the famous Armory Show in New York. There he got to know Alfred Stieglitz. In 1916 he worked on several art reviews in collaboration with Marcel Duchamp. In 1918, back in Europe, he made contact with Arp and Tzara, the leaders of Dadaism. By the following year he had settled in Paris again where he made friends with the Surrealists. He travelled a lot, particularly in Spain. During the last war, he lived in the South of France. He died in Paris in 1953.

Both painter and poet, Picabia was a great Epicurean. In 1912 and 1913 and again after 1945, his painting was rigorously abstract. Between those two periods he contributed with much originality to the *avant-garde* experiments of the day. Picabia owes his place to the vitality and restless curiosity with which he threw himself into Cubism, Dadaism, and Surrealism.

249. *Night in Spain* *1912* **p. 140**
Oil on canvas, 63" × 51¹/₈". Signed at base on right: "Francis Picabia"
Title, top left: "La Nuit espagnole", base left: "Sangré Andaluza"
Paris, William Copley collection

Pablo Ruiz Picasso

Born in Malaga in 1881. Studied in Barcelona. Made his first visit to Paris in 1900 and settled there permanently in 1904. Made friends with Max Jacob, Apollinaire, Matisse, and Braque. With the *Demoiselles d'Avignon* in 1907 he began his Cubist period. In 1911 he stayed with Braque at Céret in the Pyrénées Orientales. His first *collages* date from 1912, in which year he got to know Juan Gris. In 1913 he went to Céret again. In 1917 he visited Rome. In that year he did some work for Diaghilev. In 1920 he turned to his Neo-Classical style. Next, in association with Surrealist circles, he experimented with poetry. In 1934 he stayed for a considerable time in Spain. In 1937 he painted one of his most important works, *Guernica* – an immediate reaction to the bombing of that town in 1936 during the Spanish civil war – for the Spanish pavilion at the Exposition Universelle in Paris. During the last war he turned to sculpture, producing among other things his *L'Homme avec l'Agneau*, a figure larger than life, inspired by the Greek Moskophoros. In 1946 he was working at Vallauris, near Grasse, doing pottery amongst other things. An important part of his work consists of drawings. At present he is living at the Château de Vauvenarges.
In his early years, Picasso assimilated the elements of late 19th century art from Impressionism to the work of Toulouse-Lautrec. In 1903 he arrived at his *période bleue*, a period of veiled colouring during which he sought his inspiration in the world of wandering minstrels and acrobats. By 1905 he moved into his more serene *période rose*. It was then that he introduced us to an intimate world, softly and subtly coloured and peopled with tall figures. In 1909 his true significance for European painting began to emerge when, in collaboration with Braque, he launched into Cubism, a style that, with its new conception of space and form, was to be of capital importance to the art of our time. Picasso became the undisputed leader of modern art, yet he never rested upon his laurels. Under his influence Cubism passed from its analytical to its synthetic phase. Later, influenced by his visit to Rome, he achieved a more plastic, more expressive style. His hand succeeded at everything it touched, even Surrealism. Only pure abstraction is absent from his work. As graphic artist and draughtsman he shows a mastery which can juggle with equal ease with classic form or free expression. As a sculptor he takes one by surprise with his rough aggressiveness. In fact, Picasso has always gone straight to the heart of each successive movement of modern times, while not being afraid to jettison formulae which have served their turn. That is why his changes of style have followed so swiftly upon each other, yet they are always linked by the same impulsive reaction of his Spanish temperament to the art developments of his day. Picasso's genius dominates, as it symbolizes, the whole artistic adventure of the first half of this century.

250. *Acrobat with ball* *1905* **p. 9**
Oil on canvas, 57¹/₂" × 38¹/₈". Signed at base on right: "Picasso"
Moscow, Pushkin Museum

251. *Woman with fan in an armchair (After the dance)* *1908* **p. 112**
Oil on canvas, 59⁷/₈" × 39³/₄"
Leningrad, The Hermitage

252. *Nude in a forest (The dryad)* *1908* **p. 113**
Oil on canvas, 73¹/₄" × 42¹/₈"
Leningrad, The Hermitage

253. *Portrait of Ambroise Vollard* *1909/10* **p. 114**
Oil on canvas, 36¹/₄" × 25⁵/₈"
Moscow, Pushkin Museum

254. *Harlequin with a looking-glass* *1923* **p. 155**
Oil on canvas, 39³/₈" × 31⁷/₈". Signed and dated top right: "Picasso 23"
Izuyama, Atami-Shi, Shigetaro Fukushima collection

255. *Fishing at Antibes* *1939* **p. 33**
Oil on canvas, 79¹/₈" × 136¹/₄"
New York, Museum of Modern Art (Mrs. Simon Guggenheim Fund)

256. *Woman in a blue blouse* *1941* **p. 176**
Oil on canvas, 45⁵/₈" × 35". Signed at base on left: "Picasso". Dated centre right: "5 octobre 1941"
Brussels, Philippe Dotremont collection

257. *Two women on the beach* **p. 177**
Oil on canvas, 63" × 51¹/₈". Signed at base on left: "Picasso 56"
Paris, Louise Leiris Gallery

Filippo de Pisis (Filippo Tibertelli de Pisis)

Born at Ferrara in 1896 into an aristocratic family. Was educated in the humanities, particularly literature, and wrote poems, essays, and articles. Followed the Futurist movement for a time. At Ferrara he came in contact with Chirico and Carrà in 1916, and he joined the *Pittura Metafisica*. In 1920 in Rome he began contributing to *Valori Plastici*, and he now decided to throw himself wholeheartedly into painting. The same year he left for Paris, where he stayed almost uninterruptedly till 1940. Returning to Rome he reached his full creative period. The last years of his life were spent in a sanatorium. He died in Milan in 1956.
The aesthetic theories current in France had no real influence on Pisis, whose painting was based on tradition, going back to the 18th century Venetian school and in particular to Guardi. The old, old scenes of Venice were given a new life by an impressionistic style, lyrical and luminous, the light being rendered with a quite peculiar delicacy, which is found also in his poems. Pisis also painted numerous portraits and still-lifes.

258. *The soldier in the studio* *1937* **p. 145**
Oil on canvas, 68¹/₂" × 39³/₈". Signed at base on right: "de Pisis"
Milan, Dr. Emilio Jesi collection

Serge Poliakoff

Born in 1906 in Moscow where he was educated. Travelled widely in Russia and stayed at Istanbul, Sofia, Belgrade, and Berlin. Went to live in Paris in 1924 and attended private art-schools, completing his training at the Slade School from 1933 to 1937. Returning to Paris, he painted his first abstract pictures. In 1938 he became associated with Kandinsky, Delaunay, and Freundlich. In 1946 he joined the *Salon des Réalités Nouvelles*. In 1948 he won the Kandinsky Prize. He is still working in Paris.

though based on simple, geometrical forms, Poliakoff's abstraction may be distinguished from the colder sort and from Neo-plasticism by the richly modulated texture and warm harmony of his painting, which combine to reveal a keen sensibility.

259. Composition 1949   p. 59
Oil on canvas, 51¹/₈″ × 38¹/₈″
Paris, Prince Igor Troubetzkoy collection

Jackson Pollock

Born in 1912 at Cody, Wyoming. His boyhood was divided between Arizona and North California. Studied at Los Angeles and New York, then worked in New York from 1938 to 1942 for the W. P. A. Federal Art Project. Travelled in the United States, studying. In 1940 he espoused abstract art. In 1946 he settled at Springs, Long Island. Was killed in a motor accident at Southampton, Long Island, in 1956. An exhibition of his works was included in the 1950 Venice Biennale.
Working with an unorthodox technique, Pollock was able to give free rein to his spontaneity. He made free use of accidental affects; the colours, being splashed on or allowed to run, seem unrelated to the surface of the canvas. Forms are replaced by a fugitive, tremulous calligraphy. In the materials he used, as well as in the tools he worked with, Pollock was equally unconventional. Amongst the abstract artists who gathered around Peggy Guggenheim's Art of this Century Gallery in 1942, Pollock is the representative of a style that is the antithesis of the discipline and precision of Mondrian. Both these styles had their 'schools' in America and flourished side by side.

260. No. 2 1949   p 229
Duco, oil and aluminium on canvas, 38¹/₈″ × 189³/₈″
New York, Munson-Williams-Proctor Institute

Candido Portinari

Born in 1903 at Brodowsky in Brazil. Studied at the Academy of Fine Arts in Rio de Janeiro. His training finished, he stayed for a while in Paris, but returned to his country without having succumbed to any particular influence. Was commissioned to do a number of large murals. His work is known in Europe through the Venice Biennale. He lives at Rio de Janeiro.
Portinari glorifies the life of the Brazilian people, the cangaceiros and the vaqueiros. In his easel-pictures he probes beyond the social realism and decorative requirements of his murals. His ardent spirit expands in compositions that at times recall the art of a Goya or a Picasso in their cruel lyricism and brutal Expressionism. His work does not belong to any one country but expresses the collective agony of a period. Of wider import than Orozco or Rivera, as violent, though less of a necromancer, than Tamayo, Portinari belongs to the great current of international art.

261. The interment in the hammock 1944   p. 199
Oil on canvas, 70⁷/₈″ × 86⁵/₈″. Signed and dated at base on right: "Portinari 44"
São Paulo, Museum of Art

Odilon Redon

Born in Bordeaux in 1840. His mother was a Creole, his father a planter from New Orleans. From his childhood, which was spent in the countryside round Bordeaux, he tended to prefer solitude and dreams. But the war of 1870 stopped all that. From 1879 he began to publish collections of lithographs of a strange quality which attracted the attention of J.K.Huysmans and the Symbolists. In 1886 he made the acquaintance of Mallarmé and illustrated the works of Baudelaire, Poe, Flaubert and Verhaeren. The subtlety of his work is due to the fact that he was a visionary seeking out unknown beauties and new modes of expression. In the pastels and oils of his old age his inspiration broadens. Their mysterious poetry marks him out as a fore-runner of Surrealism. He died in Paris in 1916.

262. The Cyclops 1895/1900   p. 83
Oil on panel, 25¹/₄″ × 20″. Signed at base on right: "Odilon Redon"
Otterlo, Kröller-Müller Rijksmuseum

Auguste Renoir

Born at Limoges in 1841. Worked in Paris as a painter of porcelain, but began to frequent the Louvre and then to take lessons at the Ecole des Beaux-Arts. Between 1874 and 1877 he gravitated towards the Impressionists and contributed to their exhibitions. The years 1881 and 1882 he spent in Italy. Towards the end of his life he began to do sculptures. His first work in this field was done in 1907, but it was not till some years later that, encouraged by his friend Ambroise Vollard, he took it up determinedly. His most important sculptures were produced between 1914 and 1918. Since his hands were already paralysed by gout, he was helped by a Spaniard, Richard Guino, a pupil of Maillol. Renoir died at Cagnes in 1919.
As a sculptor Renoir showed the same qualities that had already been seen in his painting. Woman, plump and sensual, dominates his sculpture, in which the simplification of the essentially plastic elements leads him away from Impressionism. Renoir belongs to the 20th century more by virtue of his sculpture than his painting.

263. Venus Victrix 1915/16   p. 243
Bronze, Ht. 69³/₄″
Rotterdam, Boymans Museum

Germaine Richier

Born in 1904 at Grans, near Arles. Studied at the Académie des Beaux-Arts at Montpellier. From 1925 to 1929 she was a pupil of Bourdelle in Paris. In 1936 she won the Blumenthal prize for sculpture. The years between 1939 and 1945 she spent partly in Switzerland, partly in the South of France. She won the sculpture prize at the São Paulo Biennale in 1950. She has done many statues on commission, including her Christ on the Cross at the church of Assy. Lives in Paris.
Her craftsmanship is rivalled only by her uncanny spiritual energy and her extremely poetic imagination. After a period of classical experiments, 1929–1934, she felt her way towards an expressive style, with strange, aggressively lacerated forms, whose modelling sometimes recalls Giacometti. Her figures, whether animal, vegetable, or cosmic in form, take us into a magical and Surrealist world.

264. The hurricane 1949   p. 257
Bronze, Ht. 69¹/₄″
Paris, National Museum of Modern Art

Jean-Paul Riopelle

Born in 1924 at Montreal. Having received some academic training, he painted conventional landscapes while still a boy. At 17 he went to the Polytechnic at Montreal for a two-year course of mathematics. Then he went back to painting. In 1945 after reading André Breton's work on painting and Surrealism he switched to an anti-intellectual, more spontaneous style. In 1946 he settled in Paris, where he is still living. His pictures have been shown at numerous exhibitions.

Influenced at first by Kandinsky and Miró, Riopelle subsequently developed an all-embracing style and a rhythm of his own. His creative power flows out over vast canvasses in full rich colouring. His highly elaborate abstract work is based on lyrical tensions.

265. *Night* 1952   p. 229
Oil on canvas, $65'' \times 108^1/_4''$
Paris, Pierre Gallery

Diego Rivera

Born in 1886 at Guanajuato in Mexico. Studied in Mexico City. In 1907, having received a travelling grant, he came to Europe and studied at Madrid and Paris. In Paris he mixed with Cubists – Picasso, Braque, and Juan Gris – and became a friend of Modigliani. Travelled in Italy, Germany and Russia. Returning to Mexico in 1921, he was well received by the Socialist government, who commissioned a number of large decorative panels for public buildings. The work done for the School of Agriculture at Chapingo may be mentioned. He died in Mexico City in 1957.

Rivera was the pioneer of the monumental style of the new Mexican school. In a revolutionary spirit, casting off the influence of the Ecole de Paris, he developed a highly realistic art with a preference for classical form. The social and political history of Mexico provides the theme for his frescos. A great idealist, he endeavoured, with the use of primary colours and simple composition, to produce an art which would appeal to the people. Rivera has links with ancient Aztec and Maya civilizations while being skilled in European techniques, which makes him ideally qualified to be a modern interpreter of ancestral traditions.

266. *Woman rolling out pastry* 1926   p. 198
$49^5/_8'' \times 56^3/_4''$. Signed at base on left: "*Diego Rivera*"
Mexico, Lic. Emilio Portes Gil collection

Auguste Rodin

Born in Paris in 1840, son of a police official, he did a lot of drawing when still a boy, and was apprenticed to the sculptors Barye and Carrier-Belleuse. Tried to get into the Ecole des Beaux-Arts, but failed three times. Gothic art came to him as a revelation when he was working on the restoration of Notre-Dame under the direction of Viollet-le-Duc. From 1870 to 1877 he worked as a monument builder in Belgium, and he there met Constantin Meunier. Travelled in Italy and Germany. His *Age d'Airain* in 1877 attracted attention, but if he now had admirers he still had detractors. In its original form the *Burghers of Calais* was refused by that town, and literary circles denounced the *Balzac* as unrecognizable. It was not till 1900, when he exhibited in his pavilion at the Exposition Universelle that his reputation was established. He died at Meudon in 1917, leaving his sculptures to the state, and they are now kept in the Rodin Museum in Paris.

Rodin freed 19th century sculpture from the bonds of academic convention. He introduced dramatic and expressive movement, aiming far more at character and truth than at ideal beauty. The romantic grandeur of his work has been acclaimed by many 20th century sculptors, such as Bourdelle, Maillol, Kolbe, Matisse, and Lipchitz.

267. *Balzac* 1897   p. 241
Bronze, Ht. $118^1/_8''$, Wdth. $47^1/_4''$
Paris, Rodin Museum

Christian Rohlfs

Born in 1849 at Niendorf in German Holstein. Began to study in the Academy at Weimar, where he himself was soon to become a teacher. Henry Van de Velde, who was the director there at the end of the century, introduced him to the problems modern French artists were grappling with. Through Van de Velde, Rohlfs got in contact with the art-collector Osthaus, who got him appointed to the Folkwang Kunstschule at Hagen. An exhibition of Van Gogh's paintings at Hagen in 1902 impressed Rohlfs enormously and had a decisive influence on his painting. He worked for some time at Munich, returning to Hagen in 1912. From 1927 he spent some weeks every year at Ascona. He died at Hagen in 1938.

Rohlfs worked for over twenty years as an Impressionist. He was 60 when he joined the vanguard of modernism. His development is thus unusual. Having been influenced by Monet, Neo-Impressionism and Van Gogh, he finally settled down as an Expressionist. The paintings of his last years have some affinity with Nolde's, but are less ecstatic. His lyrical style, delicate and subtle, reveals and interprets nature with extreme sensitivity.

268. *Red roofs* 1913   p. 129
Oil on canvas, $31^1/_2'' \times 39^3/_8''$. Initialled and dated at base on right: "*C. R. 13*"
Karlsruhe, State Art Museum

Theodor Roszak

Born in 1907 at Poznan. Two years later his parents left Poland and emigrated to the United States. Studied successively at the Art Institute in Chicago, the Academy of Drawing, and Columbia University, finishing his training in Europe. He is now at the head of the art department of the Sarah Lawrence College, Bronxville, New York, where he has been teaching sculpture since 1941. He lives in New York.

Roszak, like Calder and Lipton, works in metals. In his early days he was influenced by the Constructivism of Pevsner and Gabo, but eventually discarded their principles, finding them limited and materialistic. If his conception of space remained the same, his forms became softer and more animated. His abstractions of organic forms are intensely expressive ornate symbols.

269. *Firebird* 1951   p. 256
Steel and copper, Ht. $31^1/_8''$, Wdth. $41^3/_4''$
Chicago, Mrs. Albert H. Newman collection

Georges Rouault

Born in 1871 in Paris into a family of furniture manufacturers. His training in craftsmanship was, however, in stained-glass work. In 1891 he became a pupil of Gustave

Moreau at the École des Beaux-Arts, where he met Matisse. In 1902 he became associated with the Fauves. In 1914 Ambroise Vollard commissioned him to illustrate some books, *Le Cirque*, *Les Fleurs de Mal*, etc. He worked for years on engraving, finishing, after much experiment, with a highly personal style. In 1929 he designed some scenery for Diaghilev's ballet company. In 1932, he went back to painting, and after 1940 used religious themes almost exclusively. In 1948 he visited Italy. The same year he designed some windows for the church at Assy. The last years of his life were clouded by a long illness. He died in Paris in 1958.

In his series of clowns, pierrots and prostitutes, painted in 1904 in dark colours and vigorous lines, full of feeling, Rouault reveals a sharpness of vision similar to that of Goya and Daumier. Eventually his moral and religious views gave his work a new bias. The powerful colours and dark thick outlines suggest the stained-glass window. Rouault's work occupies an important place in the revival of French art in the service of the Catholic church.

270. *In the salon* 1906   *p. 19*
Water-colour and gouache on canvas, 28³/₄″ × 21¹/₄″. Signed and dated top right: "G. Rouault 1906"
Brussels, Baroness Lambert collection

271. *The injured clown* 1930/39   *p. 156*
Oil on canvas, 78³/₄″ × 47¹/₄″
Private collection

272. *The judgement of Christ* 1935   *p. 157*
Oil on panel, 28³/₄″ × 41″
Izuyama, Atami-Shi, Shigetaro Fukushima collection

Henri Rousseau (Le Douanier)

Born in 1844 at Laval in Britanny. Worked as a lawyer's clerk and then as a customs officer in Paris, but retired in 1885. He then took up painting, in which he was self-taught, except for a few tips received from a couple of academic painters, Clément and Gérôme. Bouguereau was his ideal. In 1885 he contributed for the first time to the Salon des Indépendents. He got to know Gauguin, Redon, and Seurat. In 1905 he exhibited at the *Salon d'Automne*. In 1906 he was discovered by Picasso, Delaunay, Apollinaire, and Vlaminck, and in 1908 they organized a banquet at Picasso's house in his honour which has become famous. In 1909 he was implicated, quite unjustly, in a bank fraud. He died in Paris in 1910. Rousseau was also a musician. He played the violin, the trombone, and the flute, and wrote both plays and poetry. As a painter he began with naive landscapes, not in the spirit of the Sunday painter, but to earn his living. By 1896 he had acquired his own individual style, as shown in *La Bohémienne Endormie*, a big picture, both in size and conception, painted in colours without half-tones yet without harshness. Later he turned to exotic subjects and dreams. In 1905 he had a picture, *Le Lion Affamé*, in the first exhibition by the Fauves, and it attracted a good deal of attention.

Rousseau's work occupies an important place in the history of modern art. Both the Cubists and the Surrealists have paid tribute to this pure artist, and the painters of the *Blaue Reiter* group of Munich regarded him as 'the master'. Elementary forces treated with poetic imagination create a magic reality in his pictures. His example led to the discovery of numerous Sunday painters and put 'naive' art on the map.

273. *Myself – Landscape portrait* 1890   *p. 88*
Oil on canvas, 56¹/₄″ × 43¹/₂″. Signed and dated "Henri Rousseau 1890".
Prague, Narodni Gallery

Giuseppe Santomaso

Born in Venice in 1907; studied at the Academy there. His first paintings, which were representative in character, show the influence of Medardo Rosso and Semeghini. In 1939 he spent some time in Holland and Paris. Back in Venice he became, by 1946, one of the leaders of the *Fronte Nuove delle Arte*. He is still living in Venice.

His paintings, though derived directly from reality, belong none the less to abstract art. A man of great imagination, Santomaso evokes images of another world in a range of colours that nevertheless follow the tradition of Venetian painting.

274. *Green memory* 1953   *p. 219*
Oil on canvas, 47¹/₄″ × 59″. Signed and dated at base on right: "Santomaso 53"
Brescia, Cavellini collection

Martiros Sergeievitch Sarian

Born at Rostov in 1880. Studied at the School of Painting, Sculpture and Architecture in Moscow. Has taken part in important exhibitions in the Soviet Union and in an exhibition of Soviet art in India. Work by him was also shown in the 1937 Exposition Universelle in Paris, and in the 14th, 17th, 19th, and 28th Venice Biennales. He lives at Erivan.

275. *Armenian Landscape* 1957   *p. 202*
Oil on canvas, 52″ × 66¹/₈″. Signed and dated on base on right: "Sarian 1957"
Collections of the U.S.S.R.

Egon Schiele

An Austrian, born at Tulln on the Danube in 1890, he studied at the Academy of Fine Arts in Vienna, but his development was due less to that institution than to his admiration for Klimt. He was also strongly influenced by Hodler and by Far Eastern art. He served in the first war. Died in Vienna in 1918.

At first Schiele's work showed decided affinities with the *Jugendstil*. Later he adopted an expressive style characterized by a decorative delineation in which there was both mysticism and psychological insight.

276. *Woman with two children* 1917   *p. 153*
Oil on canvas, 59″ × 63″. Signed and dated centre base: "Egon Schiele 1917"
Vienna, Austrian State Gallery

Helena Sofia Schjerfbeck

Born in 1862 in Helsinki, where she later attended the art-school. Studied in Paris from 1880 to 1882, first with Bastien Lepage, then with Puvis de Chavannes. Travelled in England and Italy. Copied Velasquez at the Hermitage. In 1890 she taught for a while in an art-school in Finland. She died in 1946 in Stockholm at the age of 84.

Her delicate health obliged her to lead a very retired life. As a result, what strength she had could all be given to her art, and she was very productive, even in old age. Her paintings give a simplified version of reality – a rare tendency in the northern countries during the 19th century.

She is thus a somewhat unique figure in Nordic art, but she is now regarded as a precursor of present-day Finnish painting.

277. Woman reading 1907 p. 96
Pencil, water-colour and charcoal, $23^5/_8'' \times 16^1/_2''$. Initialled at base on left: "H. S."
Turku, Museum of Fine Art

Oskar Schlemmer

Born in 1888 at Stuttgart where he studied at the school of fine arts. In 1910 he came under the influence of Cézanne, and later of the Cubists. In 1921 Gropius employed him at the Bauhaus at Weimar and later at the one at Dessau. Held teaching posts successively at Breslau, Stuttgart, and Berlin, the last being in 1932. The following year he was obliged to retire to Southern Germany, where his painting became more and more abstract. He died in 1943 at Baden-Baden.
Oskar Schlemmer groped for a long time to find a point of balance between nature and abstraction. The *Fensterbilder* (window-pictures) of his last period show him still groping. In them the human figure appears disembodied, an extremely simplified form in Constructivist surroundings. Sometimes he even approaches metaphysics or Chirico's Symbolist dummies. He never gets away from his besetting theme, 'mankind in space'.

278. The entrance to the stadium 1930 p. 165
Oil on canvas, $63^3/_4'' \times 38^1/_8''$
Stuttgart, Mrs. Tut Schlemmer collection

Karl Schmidt-Rottluff

Born in 1884 at Rottluff in Germany. In 1905 he began studying architecture at the Dresden Technische Hochschule, and he there met Kirchner and Heckel. With them he founded the *Die Brücke* group. In 1906 he met Nolde. Five years later he settled in Berlin. He made several visits to Paris and in 1930 spent some months in Rome. In 1931 he became a member of the Prussian Academy. In 1933 the Nazis removed him, and in 1941 he was forbidden to paint at all. In 1947 he was made a professor at the Academy of Berlin, where he is still living. Besides his paintings, he has produced a considerable body of drawings.
Schmidt-Rottluff was the youngest member of *Die Brücke*. Instigated by a more elemental urge than Kirchner or Heckel, he bothered very little about spiritual problems. In this group, his work stands out by its architectural qualities. The monumental and constructive character of his compositions is accentuated by the influence of Cubism and Negro art. His work in lithography and wood-engraving have influenced his technique in painting. Using simple forms, pure colours and strong outlines, he creates a rhythm full of life. His most recent work is characterized by simplicity, but it is also closer to reality.

279. Three nudes 1913 p. 160
$38^5/_8'' \times 41^3/_4''$. Signed and dated at base on right: "S. Rottluff 1913"
Berlin, Twentieth Century Gallery

280. Forest 1921 p. 161
Oil on canvas, $44^1/_8'' \times 38^1/_8''$. Signed at base on left: "S. Rottluff"
Hamburg, Art Museum

Kurt Schwitters

Born in 1887 at Hanover. Received his art education at the Dresden School of Fine Arts. After the war he became a mechanical draughtsman. He worked for the *Sturm* group in Berlin, and was a poet as as well as a painter, sculptor, and illustrator. In 1922 he met Arp. After an Expressionist period he was drawn towards abstract art and joined the *Abstraction-Création* group. Fleeing from the Nazis, he went to Norway in 1935, moving to London in 1940. Eventually he settled at Ambleside, where he died in 1948.
Schwitters is chiefly famous for having, in 1917, created the *Merz* movement, which in Germany played somewhat the same part as Dadaism in Zürich. He also gave us his *Ursonate*, an *avant-garde* literary-cum-phonetic work. Breaking with the tradition of oil-painting, he used all sorts of odd material, including rubbish. With these miscellaneous elements he constructed his graceful abstract compositions, which in colour as well as in substance are unequalled examples of *collage* work. Moreover *Merz* symbolised the struggle of the artist against the conventional art of his day. He deliberately mixed art with non-art and with *trompe l'œil*. With that he came close to the mental attitude of the Dadaists and Surrealists, though at the same time creating a new reality.

281. Picture with red cross c. 1919 p. 147
Collage, $33^1/_8'' \times 25^1/_4''$. Initialled at base on left: "K. S."
Paris, William Copley collection

282. Rejected picture (Merzbild) – No. 31 1920 p. 146
Collage, $38^5/_8'' \times 26''$
Berne, private collection

283. Victory 1925 p. 147
Collage, $14^1/_8'' \times 10^5/_8''$
Berne, private collection

Scipione (Gino Bonichi)

Born at Macerata near San Marino in 1904. Five years later the family settled in Rome. Of athletic build (whence his pseudonym Scipione) he originally prepared for a career in sport, but this was frustrated by illness. After a period in a sanatorium he was sufficiently cured to take up painting, and he attended the Academy of Fine Arts. He exhibited in Rome in 1928, but illness was soon to cut short his career. He died in 1937 in a sanatorium at Arco.
In his brief life he rose rapidly. He became one of the leading figures in the *Scuola Romana*. Original and Expressionist, his painting, which is endowed with an Italian and in particular a Roman atmosphere, is a reaction against the academism of the 19th century. In Italy Scipione may be numbered among the most important artists of the third decade of this century.

284. Portrait of Cardinal Vannutelli 1929/30 p. 175
Oil on canvas, $52^3/_8'' \times 46^1/_8''$. Signed and dated on left towards the base: "Scipione 30"
Rome, Municipal Gallery of Modern Art

Gustav Seitz

Born at Mannheim in 1906. Studied sculpture at the Hochschule für Bildende Künste in Berlin, where he was a pupil of Wilhelm Gerstel. From 1933 to 1938 he worked in a studio placed at his disposal by the Prussian Academy. Served in the army during the last war. From 1946 to 1950 he taught at the Hochschule für Bildende Künste in Berlin. Won a national prize at the Academy of East Berlin, where he is now living.

Seitz belongs to the group of German sculptors doing representational work. The human figure is his central theme. After a journey to the Far East he did a number of portrait-busts. In his work Seitz is endeavouring to assimilate various Cubist influences.

285. *François Villon* 1952/54   *p. 267*
Bronze, Ht. 31$^1/_2$"
Antwerp, Middelheim Museum of Open-Air Sculpture

Séraphine (Séraphine Louis, sometimes called Séraphine de Senlis)

Born at Assy in 1864. Lived at Senlis, where she worked as a housekeeper. Practically nothing is known about her life or how she came to paint. Wilhelm Uhde discovered her in 1912 and gave her both help and encouragement. She died at the Hospice de Senlis in 1934.

Séraphine always painted flowers, leaves, or fruit, and she did so with startling imagination. She creates fantastic forms of great precision, the details being quite unexpected and pure invention. She never explained to anyone the technique of her glossy, richly coloured painting.

286. *Flowers* 1929   *p. 192*
Oil on canvas, 57$^1/_8$" × 44$^7/_8$". Signed at base on right: "S. Louis"
Liège, Fernand C. Graindorge collection

Victor Servranckx

Born at Dieghem near Brussels in 1897. Studied at the Académie des Beaux-Arts in Brussels. For a while he was employed as a colour-mixer in a wall-paper factory. In 1917 he gave his first exhibition of abstract painting. On a visit to America he met Moholy-Nagy, who offered him a post at the New Bauhaus in Chicago. Servranckx refused it, however, and returned to Brussels. In 1925 he contributed to the exhibition of *L'Art d'Aujourd'hui* in Paris, and he has been a regular exhibitor at the *Salon des Réalités Nouvelles*. His main field is industrial design – furniture, etc. – and he has done designs for tapestries and frescos. He lives in Brussels.

The extremely varied work of this painter falls into several currents of contemporary art – Abstraction, Surrealism, a severe form of Constructivism, and an exuberant Tachism. Servranckx has been an ardent apostle of abstract art in Belgium, both lecturing and writing on its behalf.

287. *Opus 47* 1923   *p. 210*
Oil on canvas, 44$^1/_2$" × 82$^5/_8$". Signed and dated at base on right: "Servranckx 1923"
In the artist's possession

Georges Seurat

Born in 1859 in Paris, the son of a bailiff. Studied there at the Ecole des Beaux-Arts. After completing his military service, he continued his education himself, visiting galleries and reading. Was occupied chiefly by drawing in 1882 and 1883. Made friends with Signac, and these two, be-

tween them, became the leaders of Neo-impressionism. In 1890 Seurat published his views on aesthetics and technique in a concise and almost scientific style. He led a very secluded life, completely absorbed in his work. Died in Paris of a throat infection in 1891.

At a time when Impressionism was at its zenith Seurat was groping for a more methodical and rational style, studying scientific theories on colour and optical effects. He read the works of Charles Blanc, Rood, and Chevreul. He 'divided' his colours to give them their maximum effect and this Divisionism, more often called Pointillism, is characterised by a multitude of small round touches. Signac adopted this technique, and many others followed. Painting became flatter, line took on a new significance, and colour a greater purity. Composition acquired a greater importance. In reaching beyond Impressionism Seurat was encouraging *Art Nouveau*. And with his delicate, light, luminous, and well-balanced painting, he was in many ways the true precursor of 20th century art.

288. *The Seine at Grande Jatte* c. 1880   *p. 73*
Oil on Canvas, 25$^1/_4$" × 32$^1/_4$". Signed at base on right: "Seurat"
Brussels, Royal Belgian Museum of Fine Art

289. *Sunday at Porte-en-Bessin* 1888   *p. 74*
Oil on canvas, 26" × 32$^1/_4$". Signed at base on left: "Seurat"
Otterlo, Kröller-Müller Rijksmuseum

Gino Severini

Born in 1883 at Cortona. After a sojourn in Rome, he settled in 1906 in Paris, where he has been practically ever since. He made friends with Modigliani, Picasso, and Max Jacob. After an early Divisionist phase under the influence of Seurat, he joined the Futurist movement and in 1910, at the same time as Balla, Boccioni, Russolo, and Carrà, he signed its manifesto. Later, under Picasso's influence, he experimented with Cubism and moved towards Braque's formal vocabulary. In 1922 he did some important frescos and mosaics in Switzerland and Italy. A clear and methodical writer, he has published a series of critical works and, in 1946, the first volume of his autobiography.

Severini set out to reconcile two divergent movements, one dynamic – Futurism – and the other static – Cubism. He achieved a decorative style with Cubist leanings, which later led into Neo-classicism.

290. *North-South* 1912   *p. 137*
Oil on canvas, 18$^7/_8$" × 24$^3/_8$". Dated and signed, centre base: "1912 G. Severini"
Milan, Dr. Emilio Jesi collection

Ben Shahn

Born in 1898 at Kovno in Lithuania of Jewish parents. In 1906 the family emigrated to New York, and Shahn was then brought up in the slums of Brooklyn. From 1913 to 1918 he worked for a lithographer, at the same time attending evening classes. From 1925 he spent four years travelling in Europe and North Africa. In Paris he was chiefly interested in the work of Dufy and Rouault. Returning to America in 1929 he received a number of commissions for frescos for official buildings, and in 1933 he worked with Diego Rivera on the decoration of Rockefeller Center in New York. In 1950 he taught for a year at the Brooklyn Museum Art School. In 1954 a collection of his work was shown in the American pavilion at the Venice Biennale. Lives at Roosevelt, New Jersey.

Ben Shahn is the most remarkable of the American artists of sociological tendencies. In his Realist work, he is often photographic in his detail. His work in lithography and his contact with photography have left their mark. But at times he distorts perspective and proportions for the sake of dramatic effect. His satirical side urges him to stigmatize, though with dry humour, the anomalies of the economic and political system and the horrors of war. He uses art consciously as a political weapon, and several of his works have been used for posters, though they had not been intended for that purpose.

291. Ave 1957   *p. 194*
Tempera on cardboard, 21″ × 52″. Signed at base on right: "Ben Shahn"
Hartford, Wadsworth Atheneum, Schnakenberg Fund

Walter Richard Sickert

Born in 1860 at Munich of an English mother and Danish father. The latter, A. Sickert, was a painter who settled in England in 1868, and his father, J. J. Sickert, had been a painter too. Sickert was an actor before taking up painting and he always retained his close connections with the stage. He went to the Slade and became the pupil of Whistler. In 1883 he went to Paris to hand over Whistler's *The Artist's Mother*, now in the Louvre, and by 1900 he was living in Paris, where he stayed five years. He became a friend of Degas, whom he regarded as the greatest painter of the time. He died in Paris in 1942.

Sickert painted landscapes, genre-paintings, and portraits, with a patiently matured technique, characterised by thick layers of warm colour. From Whistler he retained a preference for delicate, sometimes sombre colouring. He was one of the most influential of English Impressionists. In fact he was the most important painter between the death of Turner in 1851 and the onset of modern art.

292. Cecily Hay 1914   *p. 92*
Oil on canvas, 25¹/₄″ × 30¹/₄″. Signed base, on right: "Sickert"
London, The British Council

Joseph Sima

Born in 1896 at Jaromer in Czechoslovakia. Studied at Prague under Jan Preisler. Was an assistant at the Brünn Polytechnic. In 1922 he settled in Paris and eventually acquired French nationality. During the last war, he took part in the Resistance, and after the war he worked for a while at the Czech embassy in Paris. He went back to painting in 1947, and has since exhibited both in France and Czechoslovakia.

At first he was chiefly interested in painting on glass. Later he painted portraits and landscapes, of which he has done a large number. He likes to paint poetic and Surrealist scenes, taken from mythology, in an imaginary setting.

293. The return of Theseus 1933   *p. 191*
Oil on canvas, 51¹/₈″ × 63″. Signed and dated at base on right: "Sima 1933"
Prague, Narodni Gallery

Mario Sironi

Born at Sassari in Sardinia in 1885. After a classical education he went to the University of Rome as an engineering student, but presently dropped that subject to take up painting. Since 1914 he has been working at Milan, where he still lives. Joining the Futurist movement, he became a friend of Boccioni, with whom, incidentally, he went up for his military service in 1915. He made contact with the *Pittura Metafisica*. One of the founders of the *Novecento*, he was to remain a leading figure of the group. Between 1936 and 1940 he worked mainly on large murals and mosaics which were comissioned by, among others, the Triennale and the University of Rome. Also does sculpture.

Sironi's paintings, particularly those of the surroundings of Milan, are exceptional in Italian art in being dramatic in their expression. They combine archaistic and Symbolist elements in a way that gives them an atmosphere of modern legend.

294. Composition 1949   *p. 145*
Oil on canvas, 27⁵/₈″ × 21⁵/₈″
Milan, Cesare Tosi collection

Jan Sluyters

Born in 1881 at Hertogenbosch in Holland. Studied at a school of drawing in Amsterdam and then went on to the Academy. In 1904 he won the Prix de Rome. Besides Rome, he visited Paris and travelled in Spain. Open to the various artistic influences of his time, his painting in 1906 was a blend of Jugendstil and Fauvism. By 1910 he was turning towards Neo-Impressionism, and coming under Van Gogh's influence. Cubist influences followed in 1914. Strongly attracted to decorative work, he did posters and mural decorations, including some for the Dutch pavilion at the Brussels Exposition Universelle in 1910. After 1915 he painted a large number of portraits, still-lifes, and nudes. His palette is exuberant, his brush work lavish and free. One of his last pictures was called *The Joy of Painting*. He died in Amsterdam in 1957.

295. Staphorst peasants 1917   *p. 169*
Oil on canvas, 89³/₈″ × 81¹/₂″. Signed and dated, top left: "Jan Sluyters 1917"
Haarlem, Frans Hals Museum

Gustave de Smet

Born at Ghent in 1877. Started work in his father's studio, but later went to the local art-school. Lived a country life at Laethem-Saint-Martin, forming, with his brother Léon, Frits Van den Berghe, and Permeke, the second Laethem group (Flemish Expressionists) which was supported by the review *Sélection*. He was a member of the *Groupe des X, L'Art Vivant* and *L'Art Contemporain*. From 1914 to 1918 he and Frits Van den Berghe went to live in Holland. Returning to Belgium he settled in the Lys valley. He died in 1943 at Deurle.

An Impressionist in his early years (before 1914) he rapidly developed towards an Expressionism which at the outset was exceedingly like that of his colleagues. But his poetic feeling soon set its stamp on his work, giving it an original character. His quiet and harmonious compositions have, with their fine and graceful colouring, an idyllic and meditative character. His work is the classical Flemish example of life in Flanders as seen through Expressionist eyes.

296. The "Vogelpik" Tavern 1925   *p. 171*
Oil on canvas, 59″ × 43¹/₄″. Signed and dated at base on right: "Gust. de Smet 1925"
Boulouris, Mrs. Nelly Pisart-Fourez collection

José Gutierrez Solana

Born in Madrid in 1885 into an impoverished family of the Santander aristocracy. He began to paint very young, without any tuition. A strange and sensitive man, he spent most of his life in the underworld of Madrid and the coastal towns. During a visit to Paris, he was greatly impressed by the Musée Grévin, which gave him material for some astonishing revolutionary pictures (*Charlotte Corday*, for example). Solana has also produced some remarkable literary work, written in a bitter, violent style. In his last years his work won favour with his countrymen, and he received much official recognition, but, with his melancholy nature, his life remained as retired as ever. He died in Madrid in 1945.

Solana stands out as a remarkable personality in Spanish painting. He liked to paint country fêtes, masquerades, and popular scenes. Texture plays a big part in his work: he painted with thick layers of dark, contrasting colours with greenish tints. The expressive possibilities of line are well exploited in his drawings, which form an important part of his work. Solana's pictures reflect the miseries and hopes of the Spanish people.

297. *The bishop's visit*   p. 199
Oil on canvas, 63³|₄″ × 78³|₄″
Madrid, Museum of Modern Art

Pierre Soulages

Born in 1919 at Rodez in the Aveyron. He began to paint at a very early age and was unfamiliar with modern art. A visit to Paris in 1938 opened his eyes to current trends, but he returned to Rodez to pursue his work in solitude. Not till 1946 did he go to live in Paris, and he then exhibited for the first time – at the *Salon des Indépendents*. Since then he has been designing scenery and costumes – for Graham Greene's *The Power and the Glory* and for Vailland's *Héloïse et Abélard* among other productions. He lives in Paris.

Soulage's painting is the expression of a natural and simple strength. The massive, vigorous drawing suggests an alphabet cut down to its basic symbols. The colours are dark and the severity of the forms emphasize the structure. The delicately graded contrasts between the greys and pale colours of the background make his pictures both sensitive and dramatic.

298. *Painting 1958*   p. 226
Oil on canvas, 77³|₈″ × 51¹|₄″. Signed at base on right:
"Soulages"
Private collection

Chaïm Soutine

Born in 1894 at Smilovich, near Minsk in Lithuania, he was the son of a poor Jewish tailor. Anxious to break away from his environment, he went to Minsk, and by 1910 he was a student at the Academy in Vilno, at the same time earning his living as a photographer's assistant. In 1911 he went to Paris and frequented the Ecole des Beaux-Arts. He lived in *La Ruche*, where Chagall, Lipchitz, Cendras, and others were already installed. He made friends with Modigliani. In 1919 he went to Céret, in the Pyrénées Orientales, and stayed there for three years, working. He then returned to Paris. In 1935 he was in Cannes. He painted a number of portraits there, and in 1927 he produced his celebrated series of Choir-boys. In 1929 at Chatel-Guyon, he met M. Castaing, who became his patron and invited him to live at his house at Lèves. In 1940, times were very difficult for Jews, but Soutine managed to stow himself away in a small village in Touraine. After a short illness and an operation, he died in Paris in 1943.

Soutine, like Modigliani, was a *peintre maudit*, leading a wild, bohemian life, pursued by misadventure, but completely obsessed by his work. With little intellectual background and caring little for the fashionable movements in Paris, he painted by instinct. His passionate and visionary temperament found a natural outlet in Expressionism. Although his painting had something in it of the German Nolde or the Austrian Kokoschka, his inner vision and his attitude to life were quite different, being derived from his Jewish origin. He was able to give a new and melancholy beauty to degeneration and decay by means of tormented composition and deep rich colour.

299. *The mad woman 1920*   p. 158
Oil on canvas, 37³|₄″ × 23¹|₄″
Tokyo, Rokubin Hayashi collection

300. *The commissionaire at Maxim's 1928*   p. 28
Oil on canvas, 32¹|₄″ × 29¹|₂″. Signed at base on left: "Soutine"
Paris, Baroness Alix de Rothschild collection

Vaclav Spala

Born in 1885 at Zlunice in Czechoslovakia. Studied at the Prague Academy from which he was subsequently excluded on account of his progressive ideas. After succumbing to the influence of Cubism he joined the Fauves. In 1920 his painting went through a 'green period' and then through a 'blue period', in which he painted chiefly still-lifes and landscapes. After 1930 he enriched his palette by the addition of deeper, richer colours – reds, browns, and yellows. He died in Prague in 1946.

Spala is regarded as the most outstanding figure of Fauvism in Czechoslovakia. In recognition of his merits, he was, in 1945, given the title of National Artist.

301. *On the river Otava 1929*   p. 175
Oil on canvas, 35″ × 45⁶|₈″. Signed and dated at base on left:
"V. Spala 29"
Private collection

Nicolas de Staël

Born in 1914 in St. Petersburg. Studied at the Académie des Beaux-Arts in Brussels. After a visit to Holland, he settled in Paris in 1932. For a time he earned his living by working as a scene-painter. Stayed for a long time in Spain and Italy, but returned to Paris in 1940, when he became friendly with Braque. Eventually he moved to Antibes, where he killed himself in 1955.

Staël's abstract and lyrical style is characterised by broad architectural surfaces, painted in richly contrasting tones. After 1953 he slowly gravitated towards more representational painting while the colours were getting more and more neutral. His premature death brought to a close a career that was full of promise, and which, in any case has had its influence on many young painters in Paris and elsewhere.

302. *Le Parc des Princes 1952*   p. 227
Oil on canvas, 76³|₄″ × 38¹|₈″. Signed at base on left: "Staël"
Private collection

Graham Sutherland

Born in London in 1903. Learnt engraving at Goldsmith's College, then taught drawing and the graphic arts at the Chelsea Art School. His career as a painter only started in 1935. From 1940 to 1945 he was an official artist to the War Office. His *Crucifixion*, painted for St. Matthew's, Northampton in 1946 attracted a great deal of attention. It was followed by a series of thorn paintings. In 1952 he was asked to design a tapestry for the restored Coventry Cathedral. In the same year he won a prize at the Venice Biennale. Sutherland has done many portraits, including those of Churchill and Somerset Maugham. Lives at West Malling, Kent.

Drawing his inspiration from nature, Sutherland uses plants, insects, rocks, etc, to create a strange magic world into which his models are incorporated. His bold angular drawing is full of expressive force, sometimes creating an atmosphere akin to Surrealism.

303. *Thorns* 1946   p. 179
$49^5/_8'' \times 39^1/_2''$. *Signed top right: "Sutherland"*
London, The British Council

304. *La Petite Afrique* 1955   p. 179
Oil on canvas, $57'' \times 48''$. *Signed and dated at base on left: "Sutherland 1955"*
Private collection

Rufino Tamayo

Born at Oaxaca in Southern Mexico. Studied in Mexico City. Though profoundly impressed by French painting, he nevertheless turned back towards Mexican tradition, which he studied attentively. In 1933 he undertook some large murals for the conservatory in Mexico City, at whose art school he taught for a while. Settling in New York in 1943, he painted frescos for Smith College, Northampton, Mass. In 1950 he visited Europe, and contributed to the Venice Biennale.

Tamayo's work is more lyrical and poetic in character than that of his fellow-countrymen Rivera and Orozco. He followed the principles of the *Section d'Or*, to attain the maximum harmony and balance. In his subtle Expressionism and his delicate geometry with hints of Cubism, one sees unmistakable evidence of Picasso's influence, but the work is original both in its colouring and its versatile technique, and at the bottom of all is a foundation of Mexican folklore.

305. *Man singing* 1950   p. 178
$51^1/_8'' \times 76^3/_8''$. *Signed and dated at base on left: "Tamayo 50"*
Paris, National Museum of Modern Art

Yves Tanguy

Born of Breton parents in Paris in 1900. Served before the mast in the merchant navy. Repeatedly visited England, Portugal, Spain, Africa, and South America. Greatly struck by one of De Chirico's pictures he came across by chance at Paul Guillaume's, he began to paint. In 1925 he was introduced by his friends – one of whom was Jacques Prévert, the poet – into Surrealist circles. He joined the movement and took part in various manifestations. In 1939 he went to live in the United States, where he married the artist, Kay Sage. In 1948 he acquired American nationality. He lived at Woodbury, Connecticut, where he died in 1955.

From the start, Tanguy turned away from reality, giving everything – both objects and the themes that surged up in his mind – a figurative value. Imaginary beings are placed in illusory scenes. The titles of his pictures show the mental associations and hidden meanings that underlie them. Tanguy was one of the most original painters in the Surrealist movement.

306. *Multiplication of arcs* 1954   p. 189
Oil on canvas, $40'' \times 60''$
New York, Museum of Modern Art (Mrs. Simon Guggenheim Fund)

Simeon Afanasyevitch Tchuijkov

Born in Frunze, Russia, in 1902. Studied at the Art and Technical Workshops in Moscow. He has contributed to numerous exhibitions in the Soviet Union and abroad (Hungary, East Germany, Finland, India, China, etc). He lives in the Kirghiz Republic.

307. *Girl of Kirghir Republic* 1948   p. 203
Oil on canvas, $47^1/_4'' \times 37^3/_8''$. *Signed and dated at base on left: "Tchujkov 48"*
Moscow, Tretiakov Museum

Yukei Tejima

Born in 1901 at Kochi in Japan. Studied at Tokyo under Henrai Hidai, a calligrapher of the Meiji period. In 1937 Tejima exhibited and won a prize at an important Japanese exhibition, Nippon Suodo Bijutsuin. When the exhibition was repeated the following year he served on the committee. He joined a group of calligraphers who organised a travelling exhibition to tour Europe. Exhibited at the 1957 São Paulo Biennale. Lives in Tokyo.

In his black-and-white compositions whose elements are borrowed from calligraphy, Tejima unexpectedly approaches European abstract art.

308. *Tying a bull* 1955   p. 223
Brush design, Japanese ink on rice paper, $27'' \times 51^1/_8''$
In the artist's possession

Marc Tobey

Born at Centerville, Wisconsin, in 1890. Self-taught. Went to New York in 1911, and for some years divided his time between New York and Chicago. For two years he taught at the Cornish School, Seattle. In 1931 he came to live in England. Tobey has travelled widely in Europe and the East. In 1934 he took lessons in Shanghai from the Chinese artist Teng Kwei. Eventually he gave up his English residence and went back to Seattle, where he is still living.

Known at first as a portrait painter, Tobey turned later to abstract work, inspired by the rhythm of Chinese writing. His paintings, which are often of small size, are done in an extremely subtle style reminiscent of Paul Klee.

309. *Journey in white* 1956   p. 220
Tempera, $43^1/_2'' \times 34^5/_8''$. *Initialled at base on right: "M. T."*
Seattle, private collection

Tessai Tomioka

Born in 1836 at Kyoto. At first, adhered to the Yamato style (the traditional Japanese style of painting) but later took up the Nan-ga technique (the South China school of painting). Moved in Japanese literary circles, whose influence is visible in his work. The pictures of his last years are characterised by pale colours and dynamic composition.

310. Night rain on a mountain hut   c. 1908   *p. 181*
Brush drawing, Japanese ink on rice paper 66³/₄″ × 42″
Tokyo, Ryuzaburo Umehara collection

Nicolas Vasilievitch Tomski

Born at Ramuscevo-Novgorod in 1900. Studied at the School of Fine Arts in Leningrad. Has contributed to important exhibitions in the Soviet Union and abroad, including India, China, Indonesia, and Finland. Also at the Exposition Universelle in Paris, the New York World Fair, and the 28th Venice Biennale. Lives in Moscow.

311. Old French working man   1954   *p. 266*
Bronze, Ht. 21⁵/₈″, Wdth. 7¹/₈″, Dpth. 18″
Moscow, Tretiakov Museum

Charley Toorop (Annie Caroline Pontifex Toorop)

Born at Katwijk, near Leiden, in Holland in 1891, daughter of the painter Jan Toorop. Brought up on the island of Walcheren. Began by studying music. Travelled widely, was interested in literature, art, and architecture. In 1911 she joined a very advanced group, making friends with Mondrian, the architects Rietveld and Oud, the sculptor Raedecker, and the poet A. Roland Holst. In 1921 she went to live at Bergen-Op-Zoom, where a colony of artists had formed. She died there in 1955.
Her violent colour and the tenseness and merciless hardness of her drawing may be explained, perhaps, as a revolt against her over-cultured background, but they also show her swift grasp both of men and things.

312. Friends at a meal   1932   *p. 195*
Oil on canvas, 51″ × 78³/₄″. Initialled at base on right: "T"
Rotterdam, Boymans Museum

Henri de Toulouse-Lautrec

Born in 1864 at Albi, Tarn, of an old aristocratic family. As a result of a fall from a horse in 1879 both legs were crippled. In 1882 he went to Paris, where he led a wild life, frequenting bars, music-halls, brothels, circuses, race-courses and theatres. Drink and drugs hastened his end. He died at the Château de Malromé in 1901 at the age of only 37.
From his earlist boyhood he was passionately fond of drawing. He studied under Bonnet and Cormon. Came under the influence of Japanese prints and the painters Manet and Degas. Worked for the *Revue Blanche*. With a few quick, accurate strokes he could capture the characters of the night-life of his time, which he observed with a sharp and merciless eye. Some of them – Yvette Gilbert, Jane Avril, and La Goulue – will be for ever immortalised against their background of Montmartre and the Moulin-Rouge. The quality of his drawing was a keen stimulus to

the young men of 1900, the year that Picasso arrived in Paris from Barcelona.

313. The salon in the Rue des Moulins   1894   *p. 75*
Oil on canvas, 43¹/₄″ × 47¹/₄″. Initialled at base on left: "TL"
Albi, Toulouse-Lautrec Museum

Edgar Tytgat

Born in 1879 in Brussels. Spent his boyhood in Brussels learning to draw in the workshop of his father, a lithographer. For some years Tytgat attended the Académie des Beaux-Arts in Brussels. In 1907 he went to live at Watermael near Brussels, where he produced his first woodcuts. His works were repeatedly refused by the *Salon Triennial*, but in 1913 they were accepted by the Salon in Ghent and by the Brussels Salon the year following. He lived in London during the first war, returning to Belgium after the armistice, when he settled at Woluwe-Saint-Lambert (Brussels), where he remained for the rest of his life. He did not only painting, but also etching, wood-cuts, and lithography. He illustrated many books, besides the tales he wrote himself. He also did some designs for tapestries.
Tytgat's first works were done in an Impressionist style, and at that time his fondness for fairs, horses and travelling showmen, had already declared itself – subjects that were to remain favourites with him all his life. After the war, he developed an individual style, with naive drawing and delicate colouring. Tytgat was nevertheless too much of a psychologist to be classed among the 'naive painters'. His pictures are high-spirited and mischievous in mood. Besides fairs, they show biblical and mythological scenes as well as those of everyday life treated poetically, though with a keen sense of fun. Tytgat, who belonged to no movement, remains an isolated figure in Belgian painting.

314. Fun-fair booth   1923   *p. 194*
Oil on canvas, 44¹/₈″ × 53¹/₈″. Signed and dated at base on right: "Edgard Tytgat 1923"
Lambermont, Oscar Mairlot collection

Hans Uhlmann

Born in Berlin in 1900. Studied engineering at the Polytechnic, and then became a teacher there. He began to work at sculpture in 1925, and from 1933 to 1945 worked on metal constructions, though still practising as an engineer. He first exhibited in 1945. Since 1950 he has been teaching at the Berlin Academy. In 1953 he won the German prize for his *Unknown Political Prisoner*. Lives in Berlin.
Uhlmann's metallic structures, clear-cut and severe, are built on scientific principles, in which his engineering training is apparent. Sculptor and technologist go hand in hand, and his quiet, static style shows the influence of modern ideas on industrial design.

315. Sculpture in steel   1956   *p. 285*
Ht. 55¹/₈″
In the artist's possession

Ryuzaburo Umehara

Born in 1888 in Kyoto. In 1908 he arrived in Paris, where he became a pupil of Renoir's. In 1913 he went back to Japan and became one of the founders of the Nika-Kai group, whose object was to promote modern European art-movements in the Far-East. In 1920 he was back in France, and he also worked for a while in Italy. In 1926 he founded a new group, the *Kokuga-Kai*. Since the last war he has been several times to Europe, but is now living in Tokyo.

Umehara's very personal Expressionist style seeks to reconcile Western influence with Japanese tradition.

316. Mount Fuji in autumn 1952   *p. 181*
Drawing coloured with brush, Japanese ink, mineral pigment and gold-dust on rice paper. 42³/₄″ × 23⁵/₈″
Tokyo, Matsutaro Kawaguchi collection

Maurice Utrillo

Born in Paris in 1883. He was the illegitimate child of Suzanne Valadon and a man named Boiset, but was adopted by Michel Utrillo, a Spanish critic. As a young bank clerk, he had already begun to drink to such an extent that he had to be put into a home. It was after his recovery, in 1902, that he took up painting, under his mother's guidance. In 1903 he came under Pissarro's influence. He painted in Britanny and Corsica, but it was chiefly from Montmartre and the surroundings of Paris that he took his subjects. Alcohol continued to undermine his health, and from time to time he had to be put into a home or sent to hospital. But in spite of sickness and poverty, he went on painting until, in 1914, he began to be recognised. In the years after the war he was both famous and prosperous. Utrillo also did a number of gouaches, a medium in which he excelled. In 1926 he worked for Diaghilev. The last years of his life were calm and orderly. A few years before his death he married Lucie Valmore. He died at Dax in 1955.

Utrillo's wild and tragic life never damped his creative powers. This *peintre maudit* was a specialist in the poetic interpretation of the French town, the cathedrals of Rheims and Saint-Denis, the Paris *faubourgs*, the streets of Montmartre. Influenced at first by the Impressionists, he reached in the end a simple style of his own, which had points in common with folk realism. His best pictures belong to his *période blanche*, during which his glowing palette departed little from whites and greys. During the last twenty years of his life, his work lost something of its quality and intensity.

317. Berlioz' house c. 1908   *p. 95*
*Oil on canvas, 18¹/₈″ × 28³/₄″. **Signed** at base on right:*
"Maurice Utrillo V"
Paris, Petit Palais

318. Way to the Gare du Nord 1915   *p. 95*
Oil on canvas, 20⁷/₈″ × 28³/₈″. Signed at base on right:
"Maurice Utrillo"
Muri/Berne, Dr. W. Staempfli collection

Suzanne Valadon

Born in 1865 at Bessines near Limoges. She came to Paris very young and worked as a dressmaker, an acrobat, and a Montmartre model. She posed for Renoir, Puvis de Chavannes, and Toulouse-Lautrec. At the age of 18 she gave birth to a son, Maurice Utrillo. She began to draw, encouraged by Toulouse-Lautrec, and still more by Degas, who even bought some of her works. In 1909 she gave up drawing to concentrate on painting. She worked all her life in Paris where she died in 1938.

Suzanne Valadon's drawings are mostly of nudes, though she did a few portraits, including that of her son. She also did landscapes and still-lifes. In her paintings the colour is somewhat harsh. It is the line that dominates, strong and merciless, though nonetheless supple. Both her drawings and paintings show the same expressive force and the same sharpness of observation.

319. Nude with striped coverlet 1922   *p. 97*
Oil on canvas, 39″ × 31¹/₈″. Signed and dated, top left:
"Suzanne Valadon 1922"
Paris, Petit Palais

Victor de Vasarely

Born in 1908 at Pecs in Hungary. Studied medicine at Budapest. In 1928 he threw medecine up and took drawing lessons at the Academy. He also took lessons from Moholy-Nagy, who was campaigning in Hungary for the principles of the Bauhaus. Vasarely got to know the work of Kandinsky, Gropius, Mondrian, and Le Corbusier. In 1930 he settled in Paris, doing applied art and publicity. Since 1944 he has belonged to the group gravitating round the Galerie Denise René. Exhibits at the *Salon des Indépendants* and the *Salon des Réalités Nouvelles*. He lives in Paris.

Through Moholy-Nagy, Vasarely got in touch with the Functionalism of the Bauhaus, and set himself to acquire a constructive grasp of the experiments going on in the material world around him. His abstractions, painted in quiet, contrasting colours, are composed of cunningly arranged harmonious surfaces and clear-cut geometrical forms.

320. Horn 1955   *p. 225*
Oil on canvas, 63³/₄″ × 51¹/₈″. Signed, centre base: "Vasarely 39/200"
Brussels, Pierre Janlet collection

Jorge Vieira

Born in 1922 in Lisbon. Started life as a bank clerk. From 1944 to 1953 he studied architecture and sculpture at the Lisbon School of Fine Art. Vieira is a disciple of Simoes and Leopoldo de Almeida. He uses terra cotta, cement, clay, bronze, and iron. He has also designed some medals. In 1955 he won a prize for his *Unknown Political Prisoner*, which is reproduced here.

321. Monument to an unknown political prisoner 1953
Bronze, Ht. 19³/₈″   *p. 275*
In the artist's possession

Maria Elena Vieira da Silva

Born in Lisbon in 1908. As a girl she was already familiar with the art galleries of Europe. In 1927 she settled in Paris, and began learning sculpture from Bourdelle and Despiau, print-making from Hayter, and painting from Friesz and Léger. She painted some designs for tapestries, and did some illustrations. Eventually she devoted herself entirely to painting. In 1930 she married the Hungarian painter Arpad Szenes. Has travelled widely in Europe. During the last war she lived in South America. In 1947 she returned to Paris and is still living there.

After Expressionist beginnings, she turned towards poetic, elegant abstraction. She produces an illusion of boundless space with her remarkable mosaics of dynamic lines and touches. Her vigorous and subtle painting is the result of discipline and a vivid imagination.

322. Aerial railway 1955   *p. 215*
Oil on canvas, 62¹/₄″ × 86⁵/₈″. Signed and dated at base on right: "Vieira da Silva 55"
Paris, Pierre Gallery

Jacques Villon

Born in 1875 at Damville in Normandy, the eldest of the three gifted Duchamp brothers, the others being Marcel

Duchamp, the painter, and Raymond Duchamp-Villon, the sculptor. He was a lawyer's clerk till 1894, when he went to Paris. There he studied at the Académie Cormon. It was then that he adopted as his pseudonym the name of his favourite poet. He began to earn his living by doing drawings for satirical periodicals, such as *Gil Blas* and *Assiette au Beurre*. In 1911, under the influence of his brother Raymond he became a Cubist. Gleizes, Léger, Metzinger, and La Fresnaye used to meet at his studio, and it was with them that he founded the *Section d'Or* movement. His first abstract paintings date from 1919. Between 1922 and 1930 he did a series of engravings of modern works of art. After that began his second abstract period. In 1939 he went to the United States. In 1939 he exhibited at the *Salon des Réalités Nouvelles*. He spent the war years in Tarn. In 1950 he was awarded the Carnegie Prize. Now living in Paris.

To Villon it was given to reconcile the apparently irreconcilable – Impressionism and Cubism, representational and Abstract art. In his painting he follows a theory of his own based on Leonardo's 'pyramidal vision', a theory which led him to some extent away from Cubism. His work, which can be divided into various periods according to the colour and composition, occupies a unique position in abstract painting. In it, it is the limpidity and the pure sense of proportion which bestow a classic quality.

323. Self-portrait 1949   *p. 133*
Oil on canvas, 39³/₈″ × 27³/₄″. Signed at base on right: "Jacques Villon 53"
Paris, Louis Carré Gallery

224. A Normandy dove-cote 1953   *p. 133*
Oil on canvas, 38¹/₈″ × 57¹/₂″. Signed and dated at base on left: "Jacques Villon 53"
Paris, Louis Carré Gallery

Sésostris César Vitullo

Born at Buenos Aires in 1899. He spent all his life in Paris, where he produced his sculpture in the most complete isolation. His materials were very hard wood and granite. A large retrospective exhibition of his works was held in Paris in 1952. He died at Montrouge the following year. Vitullo's sculptures are barbaric and somewhat inaccessible abstractions. They refer to the mythology of primitive continents, with the Argentine of the *gauchos* and its epic hero Martin Ferro.

325. Gaucho's heart 1952   *p. 259*
Grey granite, Ht. 31¹/₂″
Paris, Mme. Vitullo collection

Maurice de Vlaminck

Born in Paris in 1876. His father hailed from Flanders, his mother from Lorraine. He was brought up at Chatou, near Versailles. Went in for cycle-racing and earned his living as a violinist. He was a friend of Derain's, and worked in his studio at Chatou. In 1901 he went to Paris, where he saw the Van Gogh exhibition. He got to know Matisse, Picasso and Apollinaire. In 1905 he contributed to the exhibition of the Fauves in Paris. In 1908 he came under the influence of Cézanne. Served in the first war. In the course of his long career he experimented with various styles and techniques. He is the most popular French landscape painter. He died in 1958.

Vlaminck never bothered with artistic theories. He was driven by an elemental force and a love of life, nature and music. He painted by instinct. His contact with Derain and Matisse led to a Fauve period, which was merely a transition. Under Cézanne's influence his drawing became firmer, his colouring deeper. But he left that style behind him, too. From 1915 he went through an Expressionist phase, then gradually developed a Realism characterised by sombre colouring.

326. Landscape 1907   *p. 98*
Oil on canvas, 36¹/₄″ × 28³/₄″. Signed at base on left: "Vlaminck"
Basle, Beyeler Gallery

Eugène Victorovitch Voutetich

Born at Dniepropetrovsk in 1908. Studied at the School of Fine Art at Rostov-on-Don. Has taken part in important exhibitions in the Soviet Union and abroad, in particular at the Paris Exposition Universelle in 1937 and at the 28th Venice Biennale. He lives in Moscow.

327. K. Strobl 1955   *p. 267*
Bronze, Ht. 24³/₈″, Wdth. 13³/₄, Dpth. 13³/₄″
Collections of the U.S.S.R.

Edouard Vuillard

Born in 1868 at Cuiseaux, Saône-et-Loire, but in 1877 the family moved to Paris. He lived in Montmartre and attended the Académie Julian and later the Ecole des Beaux-Arts. He got to know Lugné-Poë and Maurice Denis, and for a time he worked in Bonnard's studio. In 1889, antagonistic to the academism of the 19th century, he joined the *Nabis* (Prophets). He designed posters, arranged the programmes for the Théâtre de L'Oeuvre and illustrated some Symbolist books. In 1908 he began teaching at the Académie Ranson. He also did some work as a *peintre-décorateur*, painting a series of decorative panels for various patrons, and murals for the Comédie des Champs-Elysées, the Théâtre de Chaillot, etc. In 1930 his style began to change. He became a fashionable portrait-painter, and with that the doors of the Académie des Beaux-Arts were opened to him. He died at La Baule in 1940.

In his early days, influenced by Gauguin and Japanese art, Vuillard painted vividly-coloured pictures with flowing lines which belong to the Pre-Fauvist style. But his subtle vision and innate sense of harmony found their true outlet in quieter colours and more restrained composition. The delicate harmonies of greys and veiled half-tones make his interiors, portraits and still-lifes intensely intimate. His later work, particularly in portrait-painting, became more conventional in style and thus lost some of its interest.

328. Interior 1899   *p. 91*
Distemper painting, 23″ × 37″. Signed at base on right: "E. Vuillard 1899"
Zurich, Gustav Zumsteg collection

Theodor Werner

Born in 1886 at Jettenburg near Tübingen and studied at the Stuttgart Academy. Werner often went to Paris, sometimes staying for a considerable time, and he worked there from 1930 to 1935. In 1932 he made contact with the *Abstraction-Création* group. From 1935 to 1945 he lived first in Potsdam, then in Berlin. He joined the German group Zen 49. Werner's aphorisms have appeared in the catalogues of exhibitions. At present living in Berlin.

Werner started from Impressionism; then, having learnt all he could from Cézanne, he moved towards freer configurations, but it was not till the middle of the thirties that he found his true path in abstract art. Some of his paintings have a composition which recalls oriental calligraphy. In others it is the colour which dominates what might be described as chaotic movement. Werner seeks above all to give an effect of rhythm. He is one of the most active and authentic of the various representatives of abstract art in Germany since 1945.

329. *Astral Flowers 1951*   p. 217
Oil on canvas, 39³/₈"×31⁷/₈". Signed and dated on back:
"Theodor Werner 1951"
Mannheim, Civic Art Gallery

Fritz Winter

Born in 1905 at Altenbögge in Westphalia. He worked in the mines before going to the Dessau Bauhaus where, from 1927 to 1930, he came under the influence of Schlemmer, Kandinsky and Klee. During a stay in Berlin he made friends with the Constructivist sculptor Naum Gabo. Travelled in Switzerland and France. Became intimate with Kirchner. Under the Nazi regime, his work was declared 'decadent', and he was forbidden to paint. Served in the army during the war and was held in Russia as a prisoner of war till 1949. On his return to Germany he lived for a time at Diessen on the Ammersee, near Munich. Contributed to the first post-war exhibition of modern art in Berlin. Now living in Berlin.
Under the influence of Kandinsky, Klee, and Marc's later work, Winter's style has come to bear a certain resemblance to Hans Hartung. His abstract forms recall the darkness of the mine, the depths of the earth and its geological strata. Working in blacks and greys he streaks his canvas with bars and struts, behind which a background of reds and yellows suggests another world of light and hope.

330. *Yellow luminosity 1951*   p. 217
Oil, 29¹/₂"×39³/₈". Signed at base on left: "F. Winter"
Darmstadt, private collection

Wols (Alfred Otto Wolfgang Schulze)

Born in Berlin in 1915. Began life as a violinist. Later, he studied for a while at the Dessau Bauhaus under Mies van der Rohe. He then went to live in Paris, where he made a reputation for himself as a photographer, having a considerable success at the 1937 Exposition Universelle. During the last war he was interned in the south of France, and it was then that he began to draw and paint. He won favour with the Existentialists and did some engravings to illustrate works by Sartre, Kafka, Paulhan, etc. He also wrote poems. He died in 1951.
His painting is subtle, comprehending as it does Expressionist and Surrealist elements, which are transposed however into an emotional Symbolism which is revealed in an excited outburst of line and colour, of endless dots and dashes.

331. *Composition in green*   p. 228
39³/₈"×31⁷/₈"
Meudon, Hélène and Claude Hersent collection

Fritz Wotruba

Born in 1907 in Vienna, where he studied at the Academy of Art. He started sculpture in 1926. In 1938 he emigrated to Switzerland, where he lived and worked till 1945. He then returned to Vienna, where he is now Rector of the Academy in which he had been a student.
Wotruba's style revived sculpture in post-war Austria. He works directly on stone, and usually chooses a hard cal-

carious one, of coarse texture, difficult to handle, and he leaves it in a rough state. With their architectural and monumental character, his rugged figures are reminiscent of primitive sculpture.

332. *Seated figure 1949*   p. 259
Stone, Ht. 57¹/₈"
Vienna, Austrian State Gallery

Rik Wouters

Born in 1882 at Malines, the son of a cabinet-maker. He studied at the Académie des Beaux-Arts there, and later at the one in Brussels. In 1907 he exhibited his first sculptures at the *Salon Triennial* in Brussels. He then went to live in Brussels. In 1912 he gave his first exhibition of paintings. In the same year he went to Paris and discovered the works of Renoir, Rodin, and Cézanne. Called up for the first war, he was interned in Holland after the fall of Antwerp, but managed to work in the country round the camp at Amersfoort. An illness he had been fighting for years began to get the upper hand, and after several operations on his eyes, he died at Amsterdam in 1916.
Sculptor, painter, and draughtsman, Rik Wouters, in an artistic career of barely seven years, won an important place for himself in the history of modern art in Belgium, where he stands out as the chief representative of Fauvism. Influenced by Renoir, Cézanne, and Ensor, he developed a highly personal style, characterised by a polished technique and brilliant colouring. The study of Cézanne's work led him to a more studied composition and a more disciplined use of colour. His extraordinary creative power as a sculptor is shown as much by his dynamic works, full of *joie de vivre*, like *The Foolish Virgin*, as by the figures – *Domestic Cares* for instance – which are characterized by concentration and restraint. It was the work of Rik Wouters which, in sculpture as much as in painting, paved the way for Expressionism in Belgium.

333. *The anniversary flowers 1912*   p. 110
Oil on canvas, 39³/₈"×42¹/₂"
Antwerp, Cleomine-Jussiant collection

334. *Domestic cares 1913*   p. 244
Bronze, Ht. 76³/₄", Wdth. 30¹/₄". Signed on the base, to the
left: "Rik Wouters"
Brussels, Borough of Watermael-Boitsfort

Ossip Zadkine

Born at Smolensk in 1890. In 1907 he came to London, where he attended the Polytechnic Institute. In 1911 he went to Paris to study at the Ecole des Beaux-Arts. Came in contact with the Cubists. During the last war he was in New York, but in 1945 he returned to Paris, where he is now teaching at the Académie de la Grande Chaumière.
A great admirer of Rodin and Bourdelle, Zadkine, a representational sculptor, is first of all concerned with the expressive content of his work. With regard to subject-matter he ranges over a wide field, seeking inspiration impartially in Greek mythology (Orpheus, Diana, etc.) the works of Rimbaud, Apollinaire, or Gide, or the troubled life of our times *(The cavaged city)*. Working both in stone and wood, he produces works of a modernism which is both baroque and expressive, rising at times to a tortured and poetic vision of the world. Zadkine exerts a powerful influence upon his many pupils.

335. *The ravaged city 1947*   p. 255
Bronze, Ht. 47¹/₄", Wdth. 29¹/₂", Dpth. 23⁵/₈"
In the artist's possession